HOW *NOT* TO WRITE A NOVEL:
THE ONLY *HOW TO DO IT* BOOK THAT TELLS YOU *NOT* TO DO IT!

Forget the **How to...** books on writing; this is the book that tells you how **not** to write a novel.

Every week, agents and publishers in this country receive hundreds of manuscripts from would-be authors. Of these, fewer than one per cent will make it into print.

David Armstrong was one of the one per-centers, his first crime novel plucked from the 'slush pile' at HarperCollins and published to acclaim.

But this book is not only for writers, it's for readers, too. An A-to-Z of the disappointments, frustrations, delays, rejections – and occasional joys – of a writer's life, there's something here for anyone who's interested in what's really involved in being a writer.

'Nobody knows anything,' says Armstrong: huge advances paid for books which fail; JK Rowling's **Harry Potter** – sales to date nearly 150 *million* copies – turned down by some of the country's biggest publishers.

But with five highly-praised crime novels published during the last eight years, David Armstrong's only partly right – this is a book written by someone who clearly *does* know about the agonising road into print.

From *Agents* to *Zeitgeist*, via *Editors, Launches, Publicity* and yes, even **Harry Potter**, this is a book written by someone who really does know.

If you're thinking of becoming a writer, read it.

If you're still writing at the end of it, you'd better accept it: you're probably a writer too!

HOW NOT TO WRITE A NOVEL

First published in Great Britain in 2003 by
ALLISON & BUSBY Limited
Bon Marche Centre
241-251 Ferndale Road
Brixton, London SW9 8BJ
http://www.allisonandbusby.com

A catalogue record for this book is available from the British Library

ISBN 0 7490 0680 3

Printed and bound
by Creative Print + Design, Ebbn Vale

a&b

HOW *NOT* TO WRITE A NOVEL

David Armstrong

To Sally Kindberg

DAVID ARMSTRONG was born in Birmingham and now lives in Shropshire. He left secondary school without qualifications but later went on to read English at university in Cardiff. His first novel, *Night's Black Agents* was short-listed for the Crime Writers' Association Best First Crime Novel and since then his work has continued to receive critical acclaim. *Small Vices*, his fifth novel, was published by Allison & Busby in 2001.

FOREWORD

Why Not Be A Writer? ask the ads in the Sunday papers.

The shelves of your local bookshop are packed with *How to...* books. Books that tell you how to write a thriller, a blockbuster, an historical romance. They tell you how to plot your novel, write dialogue, create characters, pace your prose and then, having done all this, how to lay-out and package your book for dispatch to a waiting world.

They tell you to consult **The Writers' and Artists' Year Book** on how to get an agent (by having a publisher) and how to get your manuscript read by a publisher (by having an agent...); which publisher to send your manuscript to; how to include postage and packing; how long to wait before making a follow-up telephone call and, throughout it all, how to remain polite, but firm.

I've just been to my local bookshop. There are *forty-three* works of guidance and advice for writers.

Many of these books are written by people I have never heard of. Like those ads that claim success for get-rich-quick schemes, if these authors really *do* know how to do it, then why aren't they doing it for themselves?

I have several *How to write...* books on my own shelves: Andre Jute, Michael Legat, Lesley Grant-Adamson, HRF Keating, Julian Birkett et al. I also have several writers' memoirs/biographies and autobiographies: Alan Bennett, Martin Amis, Brian Aldiss, Simon Gray, Philip Larkin, Mike Leigh and John Braine.

But what I *don't* have is a *How to write/get published* ... work combined with a practising writer's account of the day-to-day business of being a writer.

So, *Why <u>not</u> be a writer?* Well, for starters, there are already far too many writers in the world. Just as there are too many books and too many bookshops. There are also lots of agents who don't want to represent you, and tons of publishers who don't want to publish your book! And, unless you're a genius, it's *very* hard: like playing the piano or learning to paint, you really have to stick at it.

How *not* to write a novel, therefore, is an A-to-Z through the maddening, infuriating, heart-breaking journey that most writers face.

But writers write. Most of us have no choice. We *have* to do it. If we don't, we're miserable. And if we do, we're miserable too. This book has been written to help you get through the misery!

HOW *NOT* TO WRITE A NOVEL: AN A TO Z

CONTENTS

INTRODUCTION

'The lyf so short, the craft so long to lerne...'
Geoffrey Chaucer *The Parliament of Fowls*

The list of books rejected by publishers is one of the few things in a writer's life to give him real joy.

There's hardly a title that hasn't been turned down repeatedly... before going on to sell in millions.

Just like the A & R man at Decca who turned down The Beatles, and the comedy executive at the BBC who claimed that no one in Britain was going to find a sitcom about an irascible hotelier in Torquay funny, there are literary agents and editors who go to bed each night knowing that it was *they* who said that **Harry Potter** just would not sell.

And these weren't shoestring operations trying to publish half a dozen titles a year from a back garden shed. No, JK Rowling's 1997 **Harry Potter and the Philosopher's Stone** – translated into forty-seven languages, total **Harry Potter** sales over 130 *million* copies – was turned down by *nine* publishers, including Transworld, HarperCollins and Penguin, before Bloomsbury signed it up.

John Creasey, founder of the Crime Writers' Association, wrote more than six hundred mystery novels under a plethora of pseudonyms, but only after collecting several *hundred* rejection slips.

Frederick Forsyth's 1971 **Day of the Jackal** – worldwide sales to date, over nine million, was rejected by four British publishers before it found a home at Hutchinson, and Erich Segal's 1970 **Love Story** (21 million copies sold) was rejected by any number of publishers before making a mint for Bantam.

Are these not stories to ease the pain of any writer as he hears his manuscript thud back through the letterbox?

Stephen King (thirty-six novels in print and sales to date in the tens of millions) collected *eighty-four* rejection slips before *Cavalier* magazine bought his short story, **Graveyard Shift,** for two hundred dollars. But at least King received helpful advice with at least one of those rejection slips – on a hand-written addendum were the words: 'never staple sheets together: use a paperclip'.

Robert Pirsig's 1974 cult success, **Zen and the Art of Motorcycle Maintenance** (three million in paperback) was rejected by 122 publishers before it found a home at Vintage. (I didn't know there were that many publishers *in* America.)

And literary/commercial judgement appears to have been no less acute way back in 1920, when at least six prescient editors declined to publish **The Mysterious Affair at Styles**, the first novel by Agatha Christie: worldwide sales to date some two *billion* in over one hundred languages.

Although her sales are dwarfed by these giants, one of the most poignant stories of rejection concerns Shropshire novelist, Barbara Pym. In 1936, her first novel, **Some Tame Gazelle,** was rejected by both Chatto and Jonathan Cape. Pym put the book aside and began a new one, **Civil to Strangers.**

After the Second World War, she re-submitted the extensively revised **Some Tame Gazelle** to Cape. This time it was accepted, and they published it in May 1950.

During the next few years, as well as working for the International African Institute, Pym published four further novels. Sales were respectable, rather than sensational, but her writing, often likened to that of Jane Austen (whose own **Pride and Prejudice**, under its original title, **First Impressions,** was rejected before – somewhat revised – being published in 1813,) was held in high regard.

In February 1964, she submitted her new book, **An Unsuitable Attachment** to her publisher. Cape rejected the book. She wrote at the time that it was like hearing that someone 'doesn't love you any more'.

And that was it. Barbara Pym, 'unloved', spent the next thirteen years sending out her rejected novel, and writing new ones, (**The Sweet Dove Died; Quartet in Autumn**,) only for them to suffer a similar fate.

In 1977, the *Times Literary Supplement* published a list – chosen by eminent literary figures – of the most under-rated writers of the century. Barbara Pym was the only living writer to be named by two people, Lord David Cecil and Philip Larkin.

The following day there was piece about it on the front page of *The Times*. A matter of weeks later, Macmillan offered to publish **Quartet in Autumn.**

TV programmes and interviews followed; the book was published in September, and shortlisted for the Booker Prize.

The following couple of years saw reprints, re-issues, numerous foreign translations, Penguin editions, rights being sold in the USA and, the ultimate accolade, an appearance on Radio Four's *Desert Island Discs* with Roy Plomley.

Barbara Pym died in January 1980.

Mere schadenfreude at these spectacular publishers' own-goals forces me to mention that George Orwell's 1945 classic, **Animal Farm,** was originally declined, notwithstanding that he had already published **Coming Up For Air, The Road to Wigan Pier** and **Homage to Catalonia** in the late 1930's.

James Joyce's **Dubliners** was rejected by twenty-two publishers before it saw the light of day in 1914.

In Joyce's case though, readers, too, were apparently lukewarm about the Irishman's achievement: a year after publication, of the initial print-run of 1250 copies, only 379 had been sold. And, of these, the author himself had stumped up for 120!

And just in case you think that publishers have learned from these costly debacles, it's worth mentioning that Zadie Smith's **White Teeth** (2000) was rejected by HarperCollins (who then entered a bidding war with Penguin for it, and lost), and that the 2002 Man Booker prize winner, **Life of Pi** by Canada's Jan Martel, is said to have been turned down by three of the country's biggest houses before finding a home at the small but respected publisher, Canongate.

Now, most of us are not Agatha Christie, Stephen King, Frederick Forsyth, Zadie Smith or even the tragically spurned Barbara Pym. But what we have in common with them, and many another published writer, is that we, too, will probably have been rejected. Many times.

I spent eighteen months writing my first book, **Night's Black Agents.**

Shortly after I'd finished it, I wanted to send it out to a publisher.

There's a very strong temptation to do this. But be aware: high on the adrenaline of a sustained period of writing, one's judgement is often less than reliable, one's critical faculties less than fully engaged.

Of course, it feels very good to have begun the work, and to have actually *finished* it. After all, it requires a tremendous amount of commitment and determination to complete 70,000 or 80,000 words of even a *bad* book. Not surprisingly, therefore, you are likely to assume that you've done something pretty good. It's in this state of near-euphoria that you might be inclined to send the book out the very next day.

And ironically, it's just this sense of belief in your book that you will need to convey to a publisher or agent. But don't squander that enthusiasm. Do nothing. Don't, under any circumstances, send your manuscript out. Put it aside and leave it alone for a while. I'd suggest – if you can bear it – a few days; preferably a week, even two. After this interval, get it out, and read it again.

Re-reading it, you may still feel that there are good things there; you'll probably experience that glow that every writer feels when he comes upon a pleasing phrase that he has written.

The plot may still make sense, the pace feel right according to the action, the characters appear well-delineated and particular.

In fact, if *all* of these things pertain, and you cannot make any structural improvements, nor smooth the prose, excise a repetition or two, delete a redundant adjective, then certainly, send it off – possibly to Faber and Faber – because truly, they are awaiting your manuscript, and you are almost certainly a genius.

If, on the other hand, you are like the rest of us, and you *are* able to make further improvements, then do them now.

Because now's the time – not for you to send the book to an agent or publisher – but for you to try and recruit an intelligent, disinterested reader to look at it for you.

Your choice of this reader is very important. You must, of course, choose someone whose judgement you respect – a 'reader', obviously – and preferably a reader who is familiar with the genre of your book.

Yes, she needs to be able to tell you the truth – that's the whole point of the exercise – and yes, you have to be able to listen to what she has to say without rejecting it out of hand.

You are *very* deeply involved with your book and you are likely to be very protective of it: but if your reader doesn't understand the plot, somehow feels that things don't add up, or that the prose sounds clunky to her ear, it is probably *she* who is right, and you would be well advised to heed her.

But whilst you need to be prepared for criticism, try to recruit someone who will be sensitive to the importance of this thing to you, and who will not ride unnecessarily roughshod over your feelings.

When you've re-drafted and polished and smoothed your manuscript, left it alone for a cooling-off period, re-read it and worked it over again; when your trusted, reliable, non-spiteful, critically-acute friend has read it, and you have absorbed and – possibly – acted upon her comments; when you have done all this, read

21

through **The Writers' and Artists' Yearbook** or **The Writers' Handbook**, identify a suitable publisher (or agent), parcel up your manuscript, and send it out.

It's exactly what I did. And back it came.

Again and again and again.

The good news – such as it was – was that the rejections were invariably accompanied by encouraging words, and helpful 'reasons' why the publishers were turning the book down: 'The crime market is very depressed at the moment ...' (Not nearly as depressed as I am, I groaned.) 'You clearly write well, but the story is a little slow for today's market...' (**Night's Black Agents**, set on the waterways around Birmingham, *is* a measured, claustrophobic story of infidelity and jealousy that leads to murder.)

Eventually, a literary agent, a friend of my brother-in-law, agreed to have a look at the book.

He was very nice about it, and offered – without suggesting that he formally represent me – to send it out.

As any budding writer knows, to have an agent on board is a major breakthrough. Agents are busy people, and they are unlikely to offer to help you unless they think there's a chance of placing your work.

He sent the book out to a couple of publishers.

And back it came.

Each of them, apparently, liked it; each of them said very nice things about it. And each of them decided, finally, 'reluctantly', that they were unwilling to offer for it.

'My' agent returned my manuscript, and wished me the best of luck in placing it.

It was heartbreaking.

For the umpteenth time, I went over it again, and tried to iron out even the tiniest bump or glitch at which a publisher's reader might stumble.

When a novelist friend pointed out a publisher's ad in the *Sunday Times* 'inviting' writers to submit manuscripts, I sent mine.

Publishers *asking* for manuscripts is the literary equivalent of soliciting for an infectious disease: it just doesn't happen.

Within a fortnight, *Select Books* wrote, offering to publish **Night's Black Agents**. Wary of a scam, I asked 'Bruce' their 'publishing editor' to send me one of his company's books. He sent **The Death of Four Presidents**, by 'Densil Barr'.

I didn't think Mr Barr's book read particularly well, but it was printed on decent weight paper, had an ISBN, and was wrapped in a reasonable dust-jacket.

The company wasn't vanity publishing – the arrangement whereby authors *pay* to be published – but there was no advance either: it was a royalties-only arrangement.

No matter, if *Select Books* in London's EC1 were prepared to put **Night's Black Agents** between covers, that was good enough for me. I signed on the dotted line.

Six months later, after *many* phone calls and one depressing visit to a barren office on windy Great Eastern Street – no secretaries, no water coolers, no leafy tropical plants here – I could see that the book was never going to make the journey from Bruce's filing cabinet to the country's bookshops.

Maybe he had run out of money? Perhaps he just liked to act like an (impoverished) publisher? In any event, I asked for, and he (eventually) returned my manuscript.

A couple of weeks later, having trawled through **Night's Black Agents** (again) I parcelled it up (again) and sent it out (again). And this time, I started (again) with HarperCollins, the very first publisher to have seen it, over a year ago now.

Two weeks later, I got a letter.

The same publisher. The same book. A different publisher's *reader*, maybe. Yes, I had repeatedly smoothed the prose, and yes,

I had tried to heed the criticism that had been offered by readers, agents and editors as they had repeatedly returned my manuscript. But, essentially, **Night's Black Agents** was the same book that it had been a year ago.

And now, here in my hand, on an autumn morning in 1992, was the letter I had prayed for.

Seven months later, **Night's Black Agents** was published.

A few weeks after that, the reviews started to appear. Amazingly, almost miraculously, the very things for which the book had been rejected were now singled out for praise. The 'lack of pace' that had made the book 'unsuitable for today's market', metamorphosed in the *Daily Telegraph* into 'prose with a slow, dark, rhythm'.

In the *Guardian*, the 'Midlands setting', frequently cited as an insurmountable barrier to publication, was now, 'unique and interesting'.

And then, out of the blue, a week or two after the *Literary Review* called **Night's Black Agents** 'a tale of crime and punishment that Zola wouldn't disown…' my editor telephoned to say that the Crime Writers' Association had shortlisted the book for the John Creasey Award for Best First Crime Novel of the Year.

Would I, she asked, be her guest at the ceremony at the Law Society in Chancery Lane the following month? *Would* I?!

Tips and Summary:

1) Don't be a writer.
2) Your book may well be good enough to be published. It may well be better than any number of books that *are* published. But as well as the many poor books that are published, and the good ones that are rejected, remember that a lot of thoroughly bad

books are rejected too. And for the very best of reasons: they really are not any good.

3) Get as much feedback on your novel as you possibly can from informed readers. In this way, although you probably need to be obsessive about your book, you won't be obsessive, *as well as* megalomaniacal and deluded.

4) Be determined, bordering on obsessive.

5) Don't kill or kidnap editors and agents who turn down your book.

6) Best of all, save yourself the heartache: don't be a writer.

ADVANCES

'Some day I hope to write a book where the royalties pay for the copies I give away.'

Clarence Dallow

It's said that Bloomsbury paid Donna Tartt just under £1,000,000 for **The Little Friend** (2002) – the southern belle's second novel, ten years after her first, **The Secret History**, was both a critical and commercial success.

Way back in 1977, Macdonald Jane paid what (then) seemed an astronomical £155,000 for Colleen McCullough's **The Thorn Birds.** The Australian-set novel sold only 19,000 in hardback in the first year, but then justified the advance by going on to sell over a million in paperback.

In the early 1990's, Ian McEwan received £650,000 for his Berlin novel, **The Innocent**; Fay Weldon £450,000 for a three book deal, and biographer Peter Ackroyd received a similar figure for his lives of Charles Dickens and William Blake.

Even people who've never read a Martin Amis novel will have some recollection of the furore that accompanied the £500,000 advance paid for his 1995 jealous author novel, **The Information.** OK, it was paid as part of a two-book deal – negotiated for him by New York agent, Andrew Wylie – but it was still a lot of money.

More recent deals that have escaped the confines of the books pages and made it into gossip columns, celebrity scandal pieces and even front page broadsheet stories, were Amy Jenkins's £600,000 deal with Hodder and Stoughton for **HoneyMoon** (2000) and **Funny Valentine** (2002). This advance was paid to the writer on the strength of a synopsis and a couple of chapters: although she had created the BBC TV series, *This Life*, and written several of its episodes, she had never written a novel.

In 2001, *Sunday Times* journalist Paul Eddy was apparently paid £1,000,000 by Headline for **Flint**, his first thriller.

I say 'apparently', because perhaps we should take some of these figures with a pinch of salt. According to a recent *Guardian* article by Mark Lawson, many of these heavily-publicised advances are themselves fiction.

Magnus Mills was widely reported to have received a one million pound advance for **The Restraint of Beasts**, (1999) his first novel. In fact, the London bus-driving author received ten *thousand* pounds. The grander sum was invented in collusion with a Sunday newspaper hack to make good copy. And, of course, it did just that: decent article, some free publicity, and extra sales for the book.

Publishing publicists, not surprisingly, are happy to inflate the sums supposedly paid simply because big figures make the news, and news of the book means sales.

Of course, no matter what publishers pay for them, most books, like most films, lose money. A bit like the adage about advertising: *50% of all we spend on campaigns is wasted – we just don't know which 50% it is.* It's the same with books. If publishers knew which books would turn a profit for them, there'd be no risk and we'd all be publishers!

While it's true that some of these big advances have not been earned back from book sales – Naomi Campbell's **Swan** comes to mind – Martin Amis's half-million pound deal looks like a bargain now.

All of this is a far cry from the £1,500 (in *two* instalments,) that JK Rowling received from Bloomsbury for her first **Harry Potter** book, or, indeed, the £25 that Sir Arthur Conan Doyle was paid for full rights to his 1888 Sherlock Holmes tale, **Study in Scarlet**.

But no matter what the amount, not every writer is happy to take an advance for an as-yet unwritten book. Baroness James of Holland Park, (P.D. James), creator of the Adam Dalgleish novels,

(**Cover Her Face** 1962; **Innocent Blood** 1980 and **Death in Holy Orders** 2001) will not accept an advance before she has written a book, saying that the pressure would be unwelcome: 'What if the publishers didn't like what I eventually came up with?' she ponders.

There have been cases where this is exactly what has happened. Hunter Davies, the author of more than forty books over a thirty year career, and husband of prize-winning writer, Margaret Forster, (**The Memory Box**, 1999) was commissioned by his publisher, Michael Joseph, (part of the Penguin group,) to write a non-fiction book, **London to Loweswater**, a journey through England at the turn of the Millennium. His publisher offered him an advance of £15,000. Davies pushed them to £20,000. They agreed, on condition that he would accept a first payment of only £2,000, instead of the usual one-third upfront.

Davies spent a year writing the book, and incurred some £3,000 in expenses.

Two months after delivering the manuscript he received a curt message saying that his publisher didn't care for the book. Naturally, he was upset.

He asked for the manuscript to be returned, *and* for his outstanding £18,000. The publisher refused, claiming that he had failed to deliver the book they wanted, and that the contract said acceptance was subject to their 'approval'.

An acrimonious battle ensued, the upshot of which was that Davies eventually received a further payment of £9,000, and the matter was closed.

The story has a happy(ish) ending though. Hunter Davies ran into the publisher of one of his other titles in Soho's Groucho club one day. Bill Campbell of Mainstream Publishing offered to have a look at the work. He liked it, paid Davies £5,000 and published the book some months later.

Davies's advice: always get as large a part of the advance upfront as you possibly can.

Problems such as the one experienced by Hunter Davies can arise because of the ever-changing personnel that are a feature of the publishing business. Someone who enthusiastically commissions your book this year might have moved to another publisher, gone on maternity leave, or have retired by next. There seems to be almost an unwritten rule that the new person in the seat of power will treat all of their predecessor's putative acquisitions with suspicion and disdain, if not outright opprobrium.

Hunter Davies's unpleasant experience made a story in the Sunday newspapers, but Joan Collins got wider coverage for her not dissimilar case.

When she delivered **A Ruling Passion** in 1991 and, subsequently, **Hell Hath No Fury,** in 1992 to Random House, as part of a four-million dollar contract, they claimed that the books were not satisfactory, and sued her for the return of their one-million dollar advance.

Ms Collins, notwithstanding the literary merits of her novels, (her contract did not include an 'acceptance' clause) felt that she *had* done the work *and* submitted completed books.

The case came to court in 1994, and Joan Collins was awarded substantial damages.

Most of us, though, are not these stellar performers, but are what is known as 'midlist' writers. This term, although often used as a term of general abuse, is actually the ninety-five plus per cent of writers who have written perhaps four of five novels, and yet have not become household names.

Until relatively recently, most publishers had several midlist writers on their books. These authors produced books which sold respectably without breaking records. The publisher's best-selling authors subsidised their midlist writers who, occasionally, would make the breakthrough and become bestsellers themselves.

Ian Rankin wrote eleven novels before he became the celebrated author he is today; Louis de Bernieres had written several novels before **Captain Correlli's Mandolin** became a hit.

However, in today's highly competitive market, it's unlikely that a publisher will continue to publish an author who does little more than breaks even. He is much more likely to be dropped.

In 1993, I was offered (and accepted, gratefully) £1,500 for my first book. I don't know how HarperCollins came up with a figure of one thousand five hundred pounds. Possibly it was arrived at after some arcane calculations based upon the fact that I was a first-time author; projected library sales (the destination for the majority of the print run of 1,000 hardbacks); and Rupert Murdoch's need to make a bit of profit after he had paid the editors, printers, warehousers and transport companies that were going to deliver **Night's Black Agents** to bookshops throughout the land.

Something like that, anyway. I was glad to accept the initial cheque for seven hundred and fifty pounds, (it's usually a three way split: a third on signing the contract; a third on delivery of the manuscript, and a third on publication. But, given that HarperCollins already had my book when we signed contracts, it was fifty per cent on signature, and the rest on publication).

Like most first-time writers, I suspect, I would have accepted an advance of fifteen *pounds*, let alone fifteen *hundred*, so keen was I to see the book in print. The money was merely a bonus, a vouchsafe of my work, sign that I was a real writer, a bona-fide author.

With some of the dosh, I put on a launch party at the town's biggest hotel. I also kept at least one of the many promises that desperate people make to themselves when they are stepping over paving stones to avoid the cracks: I donated a couple of hundred of the seven hundred and fifty quid to the ashram where my wife studied yoga.

She had been a steadfast supporter of me and my work, and I wanted to thank her.

Over the next five years, with four more titles, my advances crept up. For **Less Than Kind** (1994) I got two grand; in 1995, for **Until Dawn Tomorrow**, two thousand five hundred; for **Thought For The Day**, my last title with HarperCollins, I received the grand sum of three *thousand* pounds. OK, I never received royalty payments thereafter (the cheques you receive when – if – your book 'earns back' its advance) but, by the same token, only a very few copies of one of my titles were ever remaindered either, (i.e. returned and either offered back to the author at a knock-down price, or sold off cheaply to the burgeoning remainders shops).

It may have been only a modest number, but I think at least a few of the lightbulbs in the big HarperCollins building on Fulham Palace Road were paid for out of the profits from my four books for the company.

For my most recent book, **Small Vices**, (published by Allison & Busby in 2001) I was paid a smaller advance but, for the first time in my writing career, I have now received a couple of decent little royalties cheques. Swings and roundabouts.

People somehow imagine that if you write and publish books, you're wealthy and (probably) famous. I've written five novels, am skint(ish) and few people beyond my few thousand readers know my name.

The hardback print run for a first-time crime writer might be 1,000 or 1,500 copies. It might go as high as 2,000 or 3,000. But it's very unlikely to be more than that unless it's adjudged to be very special indeed (and will, therefore, in any case, be trailing a lot of pre-publication hype, which will, in turn, translate into some sales, even if the book's a turkey).

The paperback run might be anything between 1,500 and ten thousand.

1,250 hardback copies of my last book were printed. They retailed at £17.99. Six months after publication, my publisher told me there were only 23 copies of **Small Vices** left in the warehouse.

Unfortunately, they didn't have enough unfilled orders to reprint (that would have needed an American library order which had not been forthcoming). Frustratingly, they *did* have an order for two hundred and fifty copies from Australia, but unfortunately, the order was sale or return and, if two hundred of them eventually came back from the Antipodes, that would undermine all the profit on the book, so it looks like they're not going to have the opportunity to read **Small Vices** in Ayers Rock, alas.

So, both myself and my publisher were pleased with how the book sold. There had been no advertising and only a few reviews (although those that the book did get were pretty good).

I was delighted that the book had done well, not only because I think it's a good book, (certainly the best that I have written) but also because Allison & Busby picked up the manuscript knowing that HarperCollins had passed on it. This was not a good wicket to be batting on: 'The publisher of my previous four titles has decided that this is not the 'breakthrough' book that they wanted from me, and have therefore decided to let me go. Will you, therefore, publish me?' No, not a very attractive wicket.

But they *did* go for it, and the book, which might otherwise even now be languishing in my drawer, is in print. Of course I'm glad. And, notwithstanding Samuel Johnson's dictum that no one but a blockhead ever wrote for anything but money, the money was the least of my considerations.

Had I been unable to find a publisher for that book, it would have been very difficult indeed, even for a dedicated writer like myself (for 'dedicated' read obsessive) to have found the impetus to write another, similar book, without fearing that it, too, might suffer a similar fate.

So, yes, it's good to show a profit for the firm, and it's good to have been able to repay the faith that they had in the book.

It's hard work writing a novel, and it takes a tremendous amount of love and labour. Publishers are well aware of this fact. But they are also aware that there are endless numbers of would-be writers who are ready to accept this situation, always have done, and probably always will. It's a given; it's taken for granted. What *they* have to do is try to make a profit. It may be your labour of love, but it's their investment.

Why not take my advice: just don't do it.

Tips and Summary:

1) Don't do it.

2) If, as I know you will, you ignore my advice, write the book and, by some miracle, get a publisher to offer for it, get as much for it as you possibly can. If they've invested heavily in it, they'll make at least some effort to sell a few copies.

3) As a first-time writer, it's highly unlikely you'll be paid in advance of actually writing your novel (being 'commissioned'), but if you are ever in this position, get as much of the advance upfront as you possibly can so that, if there are problems on delivery, you are in a stronger position to negotiate.

4) Ignore no. 3 above. Many writers (myself included, notwithstanding the above) are loath to accept money for work not yet done. I would find it an unwelcome burden to have been paid already for something not yet written, especially something as tenuous as a novel.

AGENTS

How do you get an agent? By having a publisher.
So, how do you get a publisher? By having an agent...

Theoretically, given that they earn at least ten (often fifteen) per cent of your income, agents need only secure their additional percentage of the advance that they are negotiating upon your behalf for them to justify your employing them.

Christopher Little, who represents JK Rowling, presumably secured for her that £1,500 advance for the first of the **Harry Potter** books. The *Sunday Times Rich List* now estimates that his cut of JKR's literary earnings amount to some four *million* pounds per year.

But even if you are dealing with figures more modest than JK Rowling's, business negotiations are frequently onerous to conduct – after all, valuing a novel is not like putting a value on your house or your collection of stamps.

There are all sorts of questions and issues to be considered: print-run; hardback and paperback editions; large print versions; audio, TV and film options; foreign rights' editions; delivery and deadlines; author copies etc., as well as the important matter of just how much the publisher is prepared to pay upfront – the 'advance' – against sales.

OK, many of these things are pretty straightforward, and many publishers use a standard(ish) contract, the contents of which have been agreed between the Society of Authors and publishers.

But to a novice, this stuff can look as daunting as any other legal document. It's therefore generally reckoned to be less stressful to have an expert intermediary to negotiate terms for you, even if you have managed to secure an offer from a publisher without using an agent – an increasingly unlikely prospect, given that most publishers today will not even consider looking at a manuscript unless it has come via an agent – Catch 22.

Just how many author copies *are* you entitled to? What are your rights, and the publisher's, with regard to your *next* book? Which countries is the book going to be available in, and for how long?

Bona fide publishers are not in the business of trying to pull a fast one over you, and trying to short-change you for a few hundred quid on your advance. But these *are* negotiable areas and, without an agent, how can you be expected to know what your book is worth, what its print run is likely to be, and whether there'll be an American or Swedish edition?

Secondly, having an agent can be a great help in not only negotiating the terms and conditions of your contract with a publisher, but removing the potentially awkward task of dealing with your editor on both business and artistic matters.

Trouble is, it's quite difficult to actually *get* an agent these days. Yes, of course they want to represent hot new talent, but when *you* are that hot talent telephoning their office on a cold Thursday morning and asking if they'd like to have a look at your brilliant new novel, it's much more likely that they'll tell you that they're not taking on any new clients right now, as their list is full.

And even if you do get through to someone, the odds are, asked on that same telephone to outline the idea behind your book, you're likely to mumble and stutter out the plot, giving such a woeful performance that it would make **King Lear** sound dull.

But if you *can* get an agent on board – and there are all sorts, from people running their businesses from a semi in Barnsley, to big London agencies with plush offices in Chelsea Harbour who represent the biggest names in literature – you are, at least, receiving a sign of faith in your book from a professional.

And whilst there's nothing at all wrong with Barnsley, do check before you sign up with an agent which other writers he or she represents, and which books they have recently placed with which publishers. Even phone one of their authors to see what they have to say about this person/business: if the agency's legit., they shouldn't have anything to hide.

And do bear in mind that – with publishers increasingly reluctant to even look at the work of would-be authors, unless that work comes via an agency – the number of literary agencies that have sprung up in recent years (some of them with rather less than obvious qualifications to be doing the job) has multiplied.

Some of the less reputable agencies charge reading fees, as well as offering to – for a fee – edit the work of new authors. Whilst your book, and certainly your first book, might need some editorial attention, it's probably not a good idea to pay for it to be done at this stage in its evolution. Of course it's a good idea to submit your work in as good a condition as possible, but any publisher or agent worth their job will recognise quality in your work even if the book needs some revision or re-writing. If there is talent there, an experienced or sensitive agent/reader/publisher will acknowledge it.

Most reputable agents submit books to editors that they know personally, and so if you get a bona fide agent to represent you, one thing, at least, is pretty certain: your book will be read by the publisher relatively quickly.

OK, the editor will not necessarily share your agent's apparent belief in the work. It's the old equation – the agent has something to sell; and the editor is the sceptical buyer, a buyer who is being offered any number of books every single day.

So, no matter how glowing the recommendation that your agent sends with the manuscript, the editor is likely to be wary.

Most likely scenario is that your book will be returned with a polite note saying that, Yes, so-and-so enjoyed the book, but didn't quite 'fall in love with it'. He didn't feel that it was distinct enough to mark it out from other, similar, books in a crowded market. Or, possibly, that the reader found the plot weak, or the characters unengaging and the hero unsympathetic. Something, anyway, along those lines.

Your agent will then probably send it to another publisher and, depending upon the response there, decide on the next move; i.e. whether to keep sending it out, the thing borne aloft by his faith in it, or send it back to you and suggest that you make changes based on the feedback that he is getting.

Any suggestions from editors or publishers' readers are encouraging, but they are absolutely no guarantee that the book will, in fact, be improved by those changes. Possibly the contrary: changes suggested by just one (albeit experienced) reader might well lead to the book losing its distinctive flavour and potential appeal.

When **Night's Black Agents** was eventually published, the very things that it had (allegedly) been declined for were exactly the same things that reviewers found to single out for praise.

Although any thoughtful writer studies every word that an editor writes about his manuscript, unless there's a specific suggestion that the editor who wants you to make those changes will then be interested in seeing the book again, I'd be very wary of doing major re-writes.

But, of course, I also know just how hard it is not to respond to that sort of encouragement. Again, it's a good reason to have the guidance and advice of an experienced agent who might be useful in interpreting just what the editor's comments are worth.

When HarperCollins's crime fiction editor, Elizabeth Walter, wrote to me about **Night's Black Agents** in 1992, she didn't say that she liked the book so much that she wanted to buy it for the Collins list. No, her letter was much more circumspect: it was guarded and enquiring. (It transpired that she felt the book was pretty polished for a first novel, a great compliment, of course, but any polish that the novel had, had come about simply because I had tried to incorporate all of the worthwhile – in my view – criticism, and had repeatedly brushed and smoothed the prose until, I hoped, it shone.)

I was very pleased and excited to receive Elizabeth's letter and phoned a literary agent, the friend of a family relative, to ask him to read the runes of it.

He assured me that it was a 'good' letter. He knew Elizabeth (doyenne of crime fiction editors, at that time) and said that it very much looked as though Elizabeth *was* interested in publishing me.

*

In 1995, two books into my career, and my third, **Until Dawn Tomorrow** due out in a couple of months' time, I signed up for a screenwriting course at Ty Newydd, Lloyd George's former home on the Lleyn peninsula in north Wales.

The late Jim Hitchmough, TV scriptwriter (*The Bullion Boys* and *Watching*) was co-presenting the course with Val Windsor, radio dramatist and TV writer (*Brookside*, etc.).

It was a useful course, and a fruitful three days. But it was one evening in the local pub that, chatting with Jim, he told me that, with three novels under my belt, I should definitely have an agent. He suggested I contact his own TV representative.

A bit like advertising agencies, film, TV and literary agencies tend to multiply, marry and divide, and Jim Hitchmough's agent, with several former colleagues, had recently set up their own breakaway agency. Within a couple of weeks I, too, was represented by them.

I hadn't long been with 'my' TV agent when he suggested that I should really have a literary agent, too. I had lunch with a colleague of his who had a small but impressive stable of authors. By the time we were drinking our coffee, she was representing me as well.

Over the next couple of years, there were a few sniffs at the TV trough of gold, and I was even commissioned by an ardent supporter of my work to do an outline and a proposal for Carlton TV of my first two DI Frank Kavanagh novels. Unfortunately, at the very last hurdle, the project was pipped to the post by another cop drama.

(This often seems to be the case: the person who is *second* in command absolutely loves the project and wants to take it forward into production. It gets to the final high office, when the person sitting in the chair of absolute power decides to go with the *other* project – this happened at both BBC Wales and Carlton – and mine falls away.

I comfort myself with the hope that one day – and soon, surely – my backer, the person who is today's number two, will be the number one, and my stalled projects will immediately go ahead and I will become very rich and just as famous.

At gloomier moments, I imagine that maybe the person in the number two seat will remain there forever, or will simply be sacked because they keep bringing to the number one person projects which he or she does not think are 'quite right'.)

Tips and Summary:

1) Don't do it.
2) Consider trying to interest a reputable agent in your work, but make sure it's someone you can get on with.
3) Ask to see their list of clients.
4) Ascertain what it is that they can do for you, as well as your outlining what it is that you feel that you have to offer them.

AUDIO, LARGE PRINT, TRANSLATIONS ...
OR, HOW *NOT* TO GO BANKRUPT

'Only accrue ...'

Anon

Very few writers hit the jackpot with a big advance, a Hollywood deal or a TV adaptation, but any number of otherwise seriously impoverished writers get a cheque here and a cheque there which just about allows them to get by.

It is large print editions, audio versions, Public Lending Rights payments, and the occasional foreign rights translation, all subsidised by doing any talks and workshops that you possibly can, that keep the midlister's head above water. As E.M Forster might have said: Only accrue.

British people spend more on books and CDs than any other nation in Western Europe. And audio books – books recorded on tape or CD – are a growing market.

Twenty-five per cent of the population of this country is over sixty years of age. It's projected that this will rise to twenty-nine per cent within five years. Given that most people's eyesight begins to fail at between forty and forty-five years of age, a very great number of people – and an increasing number at that – are reading large print format novels, or listening to books on tape/CD borrowed from libraries or bought from bookshops.

Perhaps it was simply the fact that I was younger then, or that the market has now grown in response to consumer demands and these demographic trends, but until the last few years, I was barely aware that these markets even existed.

HarperCollins sold the rights in my first three books to a large print publisher and, as decreed in my contract, I received 60% of the sum (£750 per title) that they realised.

A few years later, when the rights in my fourth book, **Thought For The Day,** had reverted to myself – something which your contract makes clear will happen if the book is allowed to go out of print for a specified time, usually a year – I sold those rights myself to the same large print publisher.

The benefit of this is that you keep 100% of the monies paid to you, rather than sharing it with your publisher. The downside is that – at least in this particular case – negotiating independently of my original publisher, the large print publisher offered me only £600. No matter; 100% of £600 is actually a little better than the 60% of £750 that I had received via HarperCollins (£450).

Large print readers tend to be a little older than 'ordinary' readers, and when my current publisher was in negotiation with the large print company for rights to my most recent novel, **Small Vices**, there was a question about whether the strong language and sexually explicit opening of the novel were entirely suitable for this readership.

The editor of the large print version suggested that she was prepared to go ahead with the book if I were able to make a few changes.

I toned down the language, amended the graphic opening, and she went ahead with the purchase.

In general terms, my books are less sexually and violently explicit than those of many other writers in the crime market. I prefer to have violence 'off the page' and to convey the implications of traumatic acts by other means. Often, the people who criticise you for writing sexually or violently explicit scenes, or using 'bad' language, read little contemporary literary fiction, and even less in the crime genre.

Although I think there's something of a backlash these days, as readers are sated by the visceral descriptions of brutality and mutilation by writers like Patricia Cornwell and Kathy Reichs, Val

McDermid and Mo Hayder (women writers seem to have stronger stomachs in these matters than their male counterparts,) there is still plenty of gruesomely explicit crime fiction out there if that is your thing.

However, *writing*, or at least *selling* your writing, is the art of the possible, and I was prepared to tone down the language and make less explicit a murder in the opening pages of **Small Vices** if that was the price that I had to pay to see the book in front of a wider audience.

Had it been a question of the book's losing its identity, I would have had reservations. As it was, I don't think that it lost anything at all by these changes.

In truth, of course, both cops and criminals *do* swear a lot. (As do the guys I play football with, and the blokes I have a drink with in the pub.) Cutting this language for the large print edition meant that cops said 'damn' or 'bloody' when, in reality, I suspect they would have said 'fuck' or 'shit'. But, honestly, I don't think it did any damage at all to the book.

Criminals are frequently violent, and murders, which very often involve a sexual motive are, by definition, both distressing and traumatic. I abhor violence, and while to avoid it in my fiction would be less than honest, I certainly don't wallow in its gratuitous depiction.

Even having made these cuts and changes, the book was a few pages too long for the format that the large print publishers employ. My editor was grateful for the changes that I had made, and said that she was going to go ahead with the book no matter what. But she also said that it would be a real help to her if I could trim a few pages.

Yes, I'm a defensive, paranoid, protective-of-his-work author. I'm also a pragmatist who tries to see the other person's point of view. I could have entrenched, said it wasn't possible and, well, who knows what? Yes, they were going to publish the book in any event.

But what about the next one? There are a lot of writers out there, and they're all jockeying for the same publishing opportunities and deals.

If it doesn't undermine your work or destroy its integrity, why *not* co-operate?

I spent a couple of hours trimming the novel. Most of us overwrite anyway. I know I do, certainly in early drafts. But even with a finished book, there's invariably a little slack.

I lost a paragraph here, a few lines there, a little bit of filling that I didn't even know I'd got, I cut.

My editor was pleased with the changes, and really, nothing was lost. It's that easy. Be prepared to do it. Don't be precious; don't be awkward or difficult when there's no need, and then, when you *do* have a point you want to stick on, it's much more likely your view will be respected and acceded to.

Large print is one thing, but your work appearing in another language altogether is quite another.

My first book, **Night's Black Agents,** is a stand-alone novel (i.e. not part of a series – at the time of writing it, I had no idea whether I could write one publishable book, let alone a *series*).

It's a love story set in Birmingham in the 1930s with the murder of a cuckolding travelling salesman at its centre.

And yet it is this book – the only one of my novels to have been translated into another language – that is available to foreign readers.

And in which country are they able to read about a Black Country murder set on the canals of the West Midlands? In Brazil.

I was delighted, of course, when the rights department of

44

HarperCollins contacted me to tell me that they had sold **Os Sombrios Mensageiros da Noite** in Portuguese.

But I was also mystified? Why Portuguese? Why Brazil and Portugal? Why not Germany or Sweden? Birmingham must, surely, seem a very distant place to the readers of Rio di Janeiro or even those of Oporto and Lisbon.

No matter, I was pleased, and accepted my 60% of the rights sale of £750 with glee.

Unfortunately, this was not, as I hoped, the beginning of a catalogue of such sales, but the only one to materialise. I think that many of my later books were much more suitable for translation, being much more cosmopolitan. Why didn't they sell, too? My suspicion is that they weren't offered very enthusiastically. I assumed that my books were being offered in these (and other) arenas as a matter of course. But maybe I was being naïve. You hope that your work is being touted to the right people at the right places.

But of course, it's much more likely that the writers whose work is being promoted and sold in these markets (if we assume for a moment that it is no better than our own) are the writers who have been paid whopping advances in the first place. Why? Because the publisher needs that book and the rights in it to sell well to recover the hefty advance that they have paid for it.

At a mere two or three thousand pounds as an advance, perhaps I was being foolish in assuming that the rights department of my publisher was lugging a caseful of my latest books to the Frankfurt Book Fair and trying to sell them worldwide?

Also, when I was with HarperCollins, none of my books was sold to audio publishers. Again, I have no idea why this was so.

It does seems odd, though, that within a year of leaving the company, with just a couple of phonecalls and a follow-up letter, I was able to sell the audio rights in the first of my books.

Since that time the same publisher has bought four more of my titles. For a midlist writer, this is wonderful. The work is done, the book already written. To be paid *anew* for the book's appearance in another format is exceptionally pleasing.

And so – even with a few required changes – all of my published titles are now available in large print, and four of them are in audio, too. The advances have been relatively small, but the thing about being a midlist writer is that these small sums do, eventually, accrue.

If *you* insist on being a writer, once your first book has been accepted and you are, as it were, through that first door, if you then produce work fairly regularly, it is ancillary earnings like these that can make the difference between your surviving, and not.

Tips and summary:

1) Don't do it.
2) But if you really must, remember, audio and large print are both growing markets.
3) As a midlist writer, you must try to exploit these outlets for your work.
4) Don't assume that your publisher/agent is promoting your work.
5) Be prepared to do it yourself.
6) Be cooperative in your dealings with your publishers etc.

BESTSELLERS

'Nothing recedes like success.'

Walter Winchell

In 2002 Nick Hornby's **How To Be Good** was the best-selling novel, with nearly half a *million* copies sold in paperback. I'm glad. I thought it a good book that turned on a plausible and funny idea. (OK, I thought it fell away badly from page 165 until the end, but hey…)

Hornby writes popular novels that are eminently readable and his readers are not insulted with the shoddy prose and feeble characterisation of a Tony Parsons or a Ben Elton (two of the other massive sellers this year).

Not far behind Hornby was Ian McEwan's **Atonement.** This is remarkable. McEwan is a literary novelist, writing about serious subjects and he's sold 444,000 plus of the paperback this year.

Three of JK Rowling's **Harry Potter** novels are in places 4, 5 and 7 (the **Highway Code's** at number 6). Her four **Potter** books sold a total of 1.6 million copies in 2002, making her, yet again, the year's best-selling author.

Ben Elton's **Dead Famous**, notwithstanding the usual Elton 'mixed' reviews, pleased readers and sold over 345,000 copies.

Lawyer-turned-author John Grisham sold 337,000 of his new one, **A Painted House**, and the (to my mind, but what do I know) unreadable Tony Parsons managed to unload 306,000 of **One For My Baby.**

The bottom half of the top twenty has got the Dave Pelzer trio of abuse and misery, **A Child Called It; A Boy Named Dave** and **The Lost Boy,** as well as surprise seller Pete McCarthy's **McCarthy's Bar: A Journey of Discovery.** There's another Nick

Hornby, **About a Boy**, and Joanne Harris's follow up to **Chocolat, Five Quarters of the Orange**.

Sebastian Faulks, another literary novelist, is at number fifteen with **On Green Dolphin Street** (266,000) and thriller writer James Patterson creeps in at number nineteen with 230,000 sales of **Violets are Blue.**

The other three books in the top twenty sellers of 2002 are a diet book, the **What Not To Wear** TV spin-off and Billy Connolly's biography as written by his wife, Pamela Stephenson, which has sold over one and a half million copies in soft and hard covers.

These figures are fascinating, and of course represent sales that a midlist writer can only dream of – but it is interesting to note the way in which these books, being *bought* on the High Street, compare with what readers borrow from libraries.

The year for which the latest figures are available, (2000/2001) shows that, unlike purchased titles, genre fiction (romance, historical and crime,) features prominently in the top 100 most-borrowed books, with women being nine out of the top ten most heavily-borrowed authors.

The late Catherine Cookson's books hold five of those top ten positions. (The other women are JK Rowling: no's 3 and 8; Patricia Cornwell: no. 9; and Maeve Binchy: no. 10.)

The only male writer in the top ten is Dick Francis – at no. 7 – with his 1999, **Second Wind**.

Crime does very well. Although not one of the top twenty best-sellers of 2002 is a crime novel, of the top 100 *borrowed* books for the previous year, no fewer than twenty-five could loosely be called 'crime' novels.

Of the top one hundred borrowed books, a mere fifth have been written by men, whereas in the bestseller list for 2002, twelve of the twenty titles are by men.

Of the top one hundred library-borrowed novels, only two have literary pretensions: Joanna Trollope's **Other People's Children** and Louis de Bernieres's **Captain Corelli's Mandolin,** in at number 98.

Notwithstanding the one or two obvious conclusions that can be drawn: Catherine Cookson and Danielle Steel have many readers who regularly borrow from libraries but who don't go to Waterstone's to buy their (or anyone else's?) novels; more women use public libraries than men, and people buy more contemporary 'literary' fiction than they borrow from libraries, I found the figures interesting, and not a little bewildering.

To further confuse matters, given that I travel to London quite frequently, towards the end of 2002, I conducted my own poll to see what was being read by passengers on the Virgin West Coast line.

As well as the laptop workers, the shameless mobile phone-callers, the tinny Walkman players, and the newspaper and magazine readers, my poll (a stroll up and down the length of the train on several journeys) showed that nearly a quarter of travellers were reading books.

Without actually getting arrested for harassment of fellow passengers, and for the purposes of (wholly unscientific) 'research', I can report that in autumn/winter 2002, the following books were being read:

Jonathan Swift: Gulliver's Travels
Graham Greene: Brighton Rock
Richard Evans: Telling Lies About Hitler
Scott Turow: Personal Injuries
James Hawes: White Merc With Fins
The Bible
Jenny Colgan: Talking to Mr Addison
Wendy Holden: Fame Fatale
John Harvey Jones: The Troubleshooter Returns

49

Marian Keyes: Under the Duvet
Jane Green: Bookends
Douglas Adams: Hitchhiker's Guide to the Galaxy
Ellis Peters: Brother Cadfael
Stephen King: Dreamcatcher
Penny Vincenzi: The Dilemma
George Bernard Shaw: Plays Unpleasant
Isabel Allende: Portrait in Sepia
Cathy Scott: The Killing of Tupac Shakur
Ruth Rendell; Adam and Eve and Pinch Me
Anita Diamant: The Red Tent
David Mitchell: Number Nine Dream
Mark Bowden: Black Hawk Down
Stephen King: From a Buick Eight
James Redfield: The Celestine Prophecy
JK Rowling: Harry Potter and the Philosopher's Stone
Daniel Easterman: Night of the Seventh Darkness
Geoff Hurst: 1966 and all that – my autobiography
James Patterson: Beach House

The first thing that strikes me is what a catholic list it is, and that four or five of the titles are classics. The second is that, with the exception of JK Rowling and James Patterson, no one on these trains was reading anything from the top twenty best-selling authors of the year.

Oh, well.

Notwithstanding all the reading that is going on in trains (and London's tubes, an area I considered too dangerous to 'research'!) after nine years in print, with five novels published, sales of about 50,000 and library borrowings of many times that, I've yet to see *anyone* reading a novel by David Armstrong in a public place.

And apparently I'm not alone. Stand-up comedian turned crime novelist Mark Billingham's **Sleepy Head** (2001) performed very well for a first novel, and the second, **Scaredy Cat** (2002) made it to number *eight* in the fiction paperback charts. Mark lives in London and told me that he, too, had yet to see anyone reading one of his books in public. Sobering thought, eh?

Tips and summary:

1) There's little correlation between what's selling on the High Street and what's being borrowed from libraries
2) But misery always does well (see Dave Pelzer/Frank McCourt/Billy Connolly etc.).

BOOKSHOPS

'...to the big bookshop in Notting Hill ...extremely depressed by the number of books in the shop and left immediately.'

Simon Gray

One of the pleasures of being a writer, surely, has to be a visit to the bookshop? Like an athlete at the gym, the car salesman on his windy lot, this is, after all, our home from home.

Well, maybe. Of course, if you're Nick Hornby or Ian Rankin, you must be delighted that in any WH Smith's, Waterstone's or Dillons, you'll stumble over a pile of your prominently-displayed new book, and the adjacent shelves will positively sag beneath the weight of your backlist.

If you're a 'midlist' writer, though, you're more likely to creep into the store, approach the shelves with dread, and anticipate the worst.

You'll rarely be disappointed.

Well over 10,000 novels were published last year in the UK, and it often seems that only 9,999 of them are available in any bookshop that you enter.

But, hey, it wasn't always like this. When my first book, **Night's Black Agents**, came out in paperback, I'd saunter into Waterstone's, wander over to the crime shelves and, savouring the moment, slowly look up. And there it was, at last, with its moody cover: *my* book, with *my* name on the spine. That was wonderful.

But, like a lot of writers, I soon learned to fear bookshops, and these days, although I can't actually resist them, I now enter with a mixture of resignation and foreboding.

Of course, the sheer number of volumes is daunting in itself. Have you been into Foyles, or Books Etc. on Charing Cross Road? To Waterstone's on Camden High Street, Hatchards on Regent Street, or Borders on Oxford Circus? How, amidst these thousands and thousands of books is anyone going to find, is anyone going to *want* to find, *your* books?

On the crime shelves, the distinguished Margery Allingham, (**The Tiger in the Smoke** (1952); **The Beckoning Lady** (1955)), is usually followed, not by one of my five titles, but by the novels of my friend, John Baker, (**Poet in the Gutter** (1995); **The Chinese Girl** (2000)) in chunky, handsome Orion editions.

There are rarely any 'David Armstrong's' wedged between these two authors. So, why not?

Well, there are several possibilities: maybe the publisher's rep. – keen to place his bestsellers, as ever, (and who can blame him?) – didn't get the bookshop to stock even a few copies of your new/current novel in the first place.

The second scenario is that the bookseller *did* have some, but the computer on the counter, EPOS – Electronic Point of Sale – harbouring within it statistics more merciless than a failing batsman's summer averages in *Wisden*, has exposed your lack of sales, and your books, having gathered dust for a month or two, have now been sent back to the warehouse.

The third scenario is that they did have some, and they *sold* them. Perhaps someone read a review, or browsed the shelf and thought: This looks OK, and they actually *bought* one. But, alas, the bookseller didn't order replacements.

The final scenario is that they have *all* of your books. This is better (especially – heaven forbid – if you're browsing with a friend). Oh, yes, this is very nice. It's always good to see a display, after all, with your name on the cover.

But, hang on, if they have them *all*, it probably means that no one's bought *any*?

Or maybe, just maybe, people have bought a copy or two, and this efficient bookseller has immediately replaced them, just like beans and Coca-Cola in the supermarket. It's the perfect scenario. It rarely happens.

And what do I do when I see that empty space, that gap in the shelves that I would so like *my* book to be filling? Well, depending upon my state of mind and my general sense of well-being, I might submit myself to the ritual humiliation of actually speaking to the person behind the counter.

I might ask if the crime buyer is available for 'a word' or, if I'm lacking self-confidence and the wherewithal to find a tragic, authorly smile, I simply ask the young assistant if she can check whether they have my 'new book' in stock. (I've already checked the shelves, of course, and know very well that they haven't.)

She taps the keys and the computer reveals (invariably,) that No, they do not have **Small Vices** in stock. I mutter something about being the author, root around in my wallet for my business card, and 'wonder' whether she might order a few copies (on sale or return).

One of three things happens next. She either looks at me suspiciously, doubting entirely my claim to be *any* kind of writer, stocked here or anywhere else; or she might say that she *will* order some, and smile indulgently, as if pacifying some hapless soul who has escaped from the local lunatic asylum; or thirdly, she might say that she will speak to the crime buyer, as she does not have the 'authority' to order without this person's say-so. She then jots the details of my book on the smallest gummed label known to man, and places it somewhere where even I can see that it will soon shrivel, before being lost forever.

Of course, knowing that this thing has little or no chance of actually happening, I feel like reiterating my request. But this breaches all known bookshop etiquette, and may well further injure my (already hopeless) case rather than advancing it one jot. I am minded of a joke. The Queen Mother is visiting the grounds of a mental hospital when a man breaks through the cordon of dignitaries and says, most deferentially, 'Ma'am, there has been a terrible mistake. I have been incarcerated here for two years in what is clearly an administrative error. I implore you to look into this miscarriage of justice.' Impressed with the man's coherence and apparent sanity, she looks from her escorts to the patient and says, 'Yes, of course, my man, I will,' and continues her inspection of the gardens. A few moments later, a lump of wood hits her on the back of the head. The man calls out to her: 'You won't forget, will you, Ma'am?'

Of course, you want to weep and wail and scream to the bookstore assistant: 'Have *you* ever written a book? Have *you* ever tried to get a book published?'

But you don't. Of course you don't. You say nothing. You wander away, pretending to look at some of the books that actually *are* on the shelves, and eventually you leave, rather more than a little depressed.

Of course, there are perfectly good, sound, hard-headed commercial reasons for **Small Vices** – or any of my other titles – not being there. Currently, hardbacks cost about seventeen or eighteen pounds. It's a lot of money to spend on a book. (However, with petrol at nearly four quid a gallon, we could discuss the relative value of a 300 page hardback novel compared with a few gallons of fuel, a cheap shirt or seven pints of lager, but let's take it as read that books *do* cost some dosh.)

People *will* spend it to get the new Dick Francis or PD James. But the new David Armstrong? I think not. Even blessed with good reviews, most of the one or two thousand hardback print run will go to libraries. I'll sell a hundred or so myself at the initial book launch and surrounding events, and a few dozen will trickle out during the following months at talks and readings and local bookstores.

But major bookshops – with very few exceptions – will rarely stock the hardbacks of little-known writers like myself, no matter how prestigious or big your publisher.

Regrettably, for the midlist author, the tide is now, apparently, also turning against the paperback. It used simply to be the case that stores couldn't stock, (because they couldn't sell), relatively unknown writers in *hard*back.

But if a writer wasn't known in hardback, how is he/she suddenly going to get noticed in *paperback*? Unless there has been some huge publicity push, or the book has come to very wide notice (it has to be notoriety, good reviews alone won't do it) since the time of initial publication, there will not — even for an accessible six or seven pound paperback — be a queue at the bookstore till.

For some years, less commercially-driven bookshops have had shelves of paperbacks by little-known writers that were not really selling. Eventually, like some ever-spinning wheel, these books would be returned to the publisher to meet their uncertain fate.

Nowadays, some publishers have a policy of not putting many of their titles into paperback at all. It costs little more to print and publish a hardback than it does a paperback of the same title. It's reckoned to cost only about a pound to give a book a hard cover and a slip jacket. But the profit on a seven pound paperback is much less than that on the £18 hardback edition.

When my first four titles were in paperback, it meant that I would, occasionally, see them in bookshops as far apart as Penrith or Torquay. The chances of this little frisson of joy happening now have all but vanished.

There is only one place more salutary than a bookshop with many thousands of *new* titles in it, (especially when none of them is your own), and that is a *second-hand* bookshop. Amongst the faded jackets and polyester dresses, charity shops always have a few shelves of yesterday's bestsellers, and miscellaneous other titles to boot.

If you really want to confront the folly of what you're contemplating, and need to find the resolve not to go on with this vainglorious task, just spend a few minutes at the book pile in your local Oxfam shop.

There, ranged before you, at ten and twenty and fifty pence each, are the blasted dreams of myriad writers who have travelled this road before you. Five or twenty or thirty years ago, these very same people embraced the hopes and aspirations that you are embracing right now.

Some of them were even *successful.* Those 60s and 70s paperbacks were books that actually *sold.* Looking absurd with their garish, dated covers, they are wedged beside titles by writers who were then – like myself now – 'midlist' authors, people who are wholly anonymous now. It feels so foolish. These people, too, received that joyful letter, that blissful phone call. And for what? For this. The bargain box in the Sue Ryder shop.

But if you refuse to heed this advice – and I know you will, just as I ignored it in my deep hunger to be in print – before you even get to the charity shop, these days, there's another place to call.

Where do you go from Hatchard's and Waterstone's and Books etc.? You go to the *other* bookshop: to the knacker's yard of publishing. To that very charnel house of words, a bustling place of greetings cards, wrapping paper, and CDs of dubious provenance. And books. Oh yes, all sorts of books. You go, to the 'remainders shop'. As an author, your contract stipulates that you are to be given first refusal should your book be 'remaindered'.

Naturally, you buy all that you can afford. After all, you have written the thing with blood and sweat and tears, you've struggled and nursed it into print, and been paid a tenth of the minimum wage for your efforts.

But now, having been largely ignored by an indifferent public, it is being offered back to you, truly, the one person who does *really* care about it. You buy enough to send to friends and relatives every birthday and Christmas for the next five years.

But what you don't, or can't buy, ends up here.

And here, no one cares how much the book first cost, how prestigious the author, how revered the subject of this or that biography. Every title finds its real value here: the price falls, until the book sells. Off-form Reginald Hill; over-ripe Patricia Cornwell are stacked cheek by jowl with Brenda Maddox's last work of scholarship, the 'definitive' work on this or that towering figure. Twenty-five pounds six months ago, down to a fiver in the precinct store.

Celebrity; massive advances; media brouhaha; *South Bank Show* profiles, they mean *nothing* in the democracy that is the remainders shop surplus bins.

Once, when I glimpsed half a dozen copies of my second book, **Less Than Kind**, right next to a pile of Booker Prize winner, Graham Swift's **Waterland**, I did not feel chagrin, I did not feel embarrassment. No, what I felt was a swell of pride that a book of mine was on *display*. Who cares that the display is in a publishers' outlet in a Cheshire shopping precinct? It's there.

There's only one thing down from the gaudy show of the remainders shop. The author's stumped up a few quid and bought a garage-full of his novel to dump on unsuspecting friends. But there's still a couple of hundred copies that neither the outlet shop wants, nor the author can take. And they have a final journey to travel. They are destined for the ultimate ignominy. The place whose name we cannot speak for very shame: all that work, the plot, the prose, those silky words and honeyed phrases, tipped into the bubbling cauldron, rendered down to a yellowing mush, stripped and shaped and cut anew, made ready for someone *else's* words. *Pulped!*

So, if you're thinking of becoming a writer, like the TV ad used to say, don't do it, eh: just say *No*. Think of it as doing a public service. After all, not everyone feels that they can paint or sculpt or dance, so why should everyone appear to believe that they can write a book?

Every other person I know is either writing, or has written, a novel. And worse, contrary to everything I have already said about the miseries of doing it, trying to get it published, reviewed, distributed and sold, my overwhelming impression is not only that many of these writers *are* being published, but they're on the very bookshelves where *I*, in a just and fair world, so obviously should be.

We all know that there are far too many books in the world. So why not help the cause? Do the right thing. Please, don't write that book.

Tips and Summary:

1) Don't do it
2) If you're a midlist writer, avoid the deeply depressing experience of visiting bookshops.
3) If you're unpublished, visit bookshops frequently. It should cure you of your fanciful and misguided notions.

BOOKS ... TO READ, AND NOT...

'If you want to be a writer, you must do two things ... read a lot and write a lot.'

Stephen King

If any living writer has earned the right to have his views about being a novelist taken seriously, it must be Stephen King.

In his **On Writing, A Memoir of the Craft** (2000), King speaks with the authority of someone who knows what he's talking about.

Like many other writers who have been rejected, but gone on to be massive bestsellers, the sort of literary equivalents of James Dyson with his bag-less vacuum cleaner, and King Gillette with his safety razor, once the Stephen King bandwagon started to roll, it really did roll!

One of the infallible tests of an author's continuing popularity is whether his backlist is still in print. I've just visited my local Waterstone's, and every single title of King's is on display.

His most recent book, **From A Buick 8** (2002) was at number four in the charts and had sold 15,000 in hardback within three weeks of going on sale.

If you can overcome the Maine-based writer's determinedly down-home style, with its plethora of 'fuhgeddaboudits' and other irritating tics, ('that muse-guy') – as if he feels the need to constantly reinforce his blue collar credentials – this is a book that's well worth any would-be writer reading. There are, after all, on the inside covers, pictures of 32 of King's books. Not all of them have been as successful as **Misery** (1987), **Carrie** (1973) and **Christine** (1983), but you'll know most of the titles, and even if you haven't read **The Girl Who Loved Tom Gordon** (2000) or **The Drawing of the Three**, (1987) odds are, you probably know a King aficionado who has.

Really, no matter what you think of his novels – and I became interested in him when I realised that the only titles of his I'd read (**Misery** and **The Shining** 1977), were actually about *being* a writer – it's probably worth listening to any author who has been as successful as King.

For eight *years* King collected rejection slips from journals like *Alfred Hitchcock's Mystery Magazine* before he finally got an acceptance.

And even the euphoria following the phone call from his soon-to-be agent, 'Did you write this? I'm gonna make you rich…' was actually followed by many more rejections before he made the real breakthrough.

King attributes his own success to two things: a 'serene atmosphere' that allows him to write 2,000 words a day; and a 'stable relationship with a self-reliant woman …'

His wife (rather disconcertingly referred to as 'Tabby' throughout the book), 'never voiced a single doubt' about his writing, either when he was doing a succession of menial jobs to pay the rent or, later, when he was battling booze and drugs. (Just to complete the rock star analogy, King now plays in a band with other writers, including Amy Tan.)

He subsequently used the experience of those hopeless jobs as material for his fiction: the summer holiday janitor who, cleaning the girls' lavatories, links the sanitary 'napkin dispenser' with the idea of an isolated, picked-on girl at school, the inspired connection that became his first novel, **Carrie.**

King is good at conveying the excitement that a writer feels when he stumbles upon an idea that might work, and the boundless joy of finally getting an acceptance. Doubleday offered $2,500 for the hardback rights to **Carrie**. And, like almost every other successful writer in history, although he makes it clear that he doesn't do it *for* the money, he was certainly pretty chuffed when, a year later, the paperback rights were sold for $400,000.

Just to add a little spice to the tale, he reminds us that the three page outline for his first best-selling book had to be rescued from the bin by his wife after he had given up on it!

But there's not much wishy-washy sentimentality here. King's too pragmatic to pull his punches about what he feels can, and cannot, be achieved by any writer, notwithstanding their discipline, determination or anything else. He summarises it thus: '…it is impossible to make a competent writer out of a bad writer, and while it is equally impossible to make a great writer out of a good one, it *is* possible to make a good writer out of a merely competent one.'

One of the many practical tips that King offers to would-be writers is that they should always be ready to jot down an idea, no matter how inconvenient the time and place.

After falling asleep on a transatlantic flight, he noted down on a cocktail napkin his dream. Later, in a London hotel, jet-lagged and unable to sleep, he wrote the sixteen-page outline of the story of that dream which became the novel, **Misery**.

Misery is not only a wonderful idea about the 'redemptive power of writing' but, unlike some of the author's other books, the story is *plausible*. Extraordinary, yes, but it *could* be true. Of course Annie Wilkes doesn't represent the behaviour of a normal woman, but the fact that Lady Macbeth isn't 'normal' doesn't mean her behaviour is not credible.

Like most writers, Stephen King knows just how important a good idea is, and when he gets one, he certainly goes to work. The first draft of **The Running Man** (1982) took him only a week, and he suggests that first drafts of even long books should take no more than three months. Longer than this, and 'the excitement of spinning something new begins to fade'.

Although the Stephen King of **On Writing** is pretty modest, I don't think he's been well-advised to include examples of the evolution of first to second draft work. You'd need to be even more of a writing anorak than me (and I'm pretty dysfunctional in this area) to want to compare line for line deletions and amendments in pages of a King novel. King's a very successful writer, but he's not Henry James.

Not surprisingly, perhaps, having been very nearly killed while out on his afternoon walk – an activity generally recommended for writers, but *do* avoid pick-ups driven by men with boisterous rotweillers in the cab – King includes the account of his terrible accident and subsequent recovery in the book.

When the case eventually comes to court, King drily notes that Bryan Smith – who had a string of previous driving offences – receives a six month *suspended* jail term, is banned from driving for a year and will, in future, only be able to drive vehicles such as *snowmobiles* under certain 'restrictions'.

As it turned out, neither snowmobiles nor any other vehicles were to feature in Bryan Smith's life. In September of 2000, the man was found dead in his trailer.

'As of this writing,' says King, 'the cause of his death remains undetermined.'

Of the hundreds of books that deal with, or touch upon, writing, I'll suggest just half a dozen others that I've found useful or particularly enjoyed:

Dorothea Brande: Becoming a Writer (1934, but now reissued by Macmillan at £9.99) The best book about actually dealing with *writing* that I've ever read.

Carole Blake: From Pitch to Publication (Macmillan, 1999) The inside track: an agent's view of the business; informative and very readable.

Jeremy Lewis: Kindred Spirits (HarperCollins, 1995) An idiosyncratic account of the author's life in publishing. Funny and tender, a charming book with some of the longest sentences I've read since George Eliot.

The Paris Review Interviews: Writers at work. (Penguin) Invaluable insight into vast array of writers and their working methods. Essential reading for writer-groupies.

Philip Larkin: Required Writing (Faber and Faber, 1983) Droll essays on lots of writing-related matters.

Simon Gray: An Unnatural Pursuit (1985); **Enter a Fox** (2001); **Fat Chance** (1995) all Faber and Faber. The paranoid writer's essential companion. Playwright, novelist and screenwriter Simon Gray is convinced that almost everything is bad. Comfortingly for writers like myself, he's invariably right.

COURSES

'When amateur writers get together, they talk about plot and style; when professional writers meet, they talk about royalties...'

Anon

Some people peer through the wire mesh to watch their football team training; others queue for hours to get near to their film or pop idols. Me, I savour the aroma of people who write. If you're a writer-groupie, you'll sign up for more or less anything that involves other authors.

But beware: writing courses are a very mixed bag. Just like the *How To...* books that claim the author has the secrets which will enable *you* to write a bestseller, courses are frequently tutored by people you have never heard of. Like afternoon soap actors turning up on *Richard and Judy*, with their hoary anecdotes and made-up faces, their day has often been and gone.

Of course, it's not necessarily true that just because someone is not well-known that they have nothing to teach an aspiring writer. Fashions change, people come and go and, as ever, talent does, sometimes, go unrecognised.

I think that you learn to write by having some talent for it, some notion of how to put words together. And apart from that, writers *write*. Again and again and again. Writing is re-writing. Like being a good carpenter or bricklayer or footballer, as you practise and do it more, you get better. And one of the ways in which you get better is by watching other bricklayers build their walls, carpenters cut and chisel their joints, or footballers dribble past defenders.

But there does seem to be a market for tuition. The weekend

newspapers frequently run advertisements that pose the rhetorical question: *Do you want to be a writer?* which invite readers to subscribe to this magazine or that correspondence course that will help them on their way. Some go so far as to guarantee to refund the fee if the cost of the subscription has not been earned back from selling material by the end of the course.

There's even software for your computer which invites you to write a novel: '***Newnovelist*** *makes the rewarding process of writing a novel both easy and fun…*' 'Easy and fun …' eh? We should be so lucky!

As any published writer will tell you, would-be writers are keen to tell published authors about *their* work in progress (or planning). If you are as generous with your time as you should be (given that others have often done the same for you along the route to print) you will hear about these writers' books.

But, to be brutally honest, one of the things that invariably assures me that the person I'm speaking to will *never* be published, is when they do this.

Would-be writers need to be driven and focused, but they should avoid talking about their book, and get on with actually *writing* it.

Of course you need guidance and help and suggestions, but what you shouldn't do is endlessly talk about your idea instead of doing the much more difficult thing of sitting at home and writing it.

I have often been cornered by people who give me *very* detailed information about the plot and characters that they have forming in their minds. This talking *about* writing takes away the thrill and excitement of actually doing it. As far as the subconscious is concerned, if you talk the book out, it is already 'written': you come to write it, and it will be flat, used, and uninspiring (see Dorothea Brande's **Becoming a Writer**).

*

The other thing that makes me wary of the person who talks for as long as you will allow them about themselves and their work, is when that person makes no reference to any other writer.

A bit like those people who tell you they are going to write a TV sitcom, because 'there's nothing on TV these days'; they often either don't actually know what *is* on, or are living in a never-never land that they seem to think only spawned classic shows like *Only Fools and Horses*, *Dad's Army*, *Fawlty Towers* and *Blackadder*.

Those shows were the exception. They are the ones that we revere and remember because they were the exception to the rule. The thousand other routine efforts have long been forgotten. Know your market, and be aware of what's going on in that market.

If you are going to attend a course or workshop given by another writer, mere courtesy suggests to me that you should at least have a passing acquaintance with that writer's books. Take the time to find out about the person you are going to listen to. Apart from anything else, it'll give you a notion of whether you really *do* want to heed what they have to say.

Having said this, I am not suggesting that you should read everything in the genre in which you intend to write. You would be swamped and overwhelmed. You would absorb other people's style and tics, lose your own 'voice' in the process and anyway, probably be so daunted by the quality of what you read that you'd never switch on your word-processor again. (This might, of course, be a good thing but, given that you are reading this book, I suspect that you are beyond that kind of help.)

When my first book was accepted, I confided to my then-editor that I had read relatively little crime fiction. She said that I should concentrate on my own style, and not be unduly influenced by others. She wasn't suggesting that I should not read other crime writers, but that I didn't need to feel inferior in ploughing my own particular furrow.

I suppose there have been occasions where I have possibly strayed into a plot area that, had I been more familiar with the work of others in the field, I would have eschewed.

But the counter to that argument is the oft-repeated notion that there are only seven basic plots in the world anyway, and so it is the *spin* that a writer puts on them that is the important thing, not the actual plot itself. Neither Shakespeare nor Chaucer had qualms about borrowing other writers' plots. They simply took the base metal that they found, and worked their alchemy.

Tips and Summary:

1) Don't do courses, they'll only encourage you.

2) If you must attend courses, don't talk your work out; write it.

3) Be aware of what's going on in the area of literature you're interested in.

1) Read up on the person/people giving the course – it's polite, and it'll also tell you whether you rate their advice.

COVERS

'I'm not saying all publishers have to be literary, but some *interest in books would help.'*

AN Wilson

Slip jackets (on hardbacks) were originally used simply to protect the book until it was home in the purchaser's library. To have left it on would have been about as vulgar as leaving the plastic covers on the seats of your new Vauxhall Corsa: yes, it might increase the resale value in five years' time, but come on!

Your contract will probably say something about being 'consulted' about the cover for your book. In reality, the art department will come up with something based on a reading of the blurb, (which it's very likely that you will have been asked to write) and you will be expected simply to 'approve' it.

With my first four novels, I received the artwork in the post, and it was more or less a fait accompli. The implication being: we absolutely love this, and we're sure you will, too.

In fact, you are probably so delighted to see your name on what is going to be the cover of *your* book, that you would accept more or less anything. Several people will have spent time working on your project, and it would seem churlish not to share their enthusiasm for the cover, even if you are actually less than happy about it.

They may not have the commitment to your book that you do but, on the other hand, they do publish lots of other books, and so, although no one has the emotional commitment to the work that the author does, the publishers *do* have a lot of experience.

And anyway, you are in a vulnerable position: you *are* being published, and you probably feel privileged to be being so, there are, after all, many writers who would wish to be in your shoes right now – so don't rock the boat.

Both booksellers and readers are, of course, heavily influenced by jacket design. The average book buyer takes little more than one second to decide which book to pick up and browse, and that decision is made largely on the basis of the cover.

Keen to influence the biggest book retailer of them all, it is not unusual for publishers to consult with WH Smith about jacket design and, on occasions, actually change a cover at their request.

Possibly, later, when you are a bestseller, you will be invited to sit in on the sort of conferences that take place about the cover for the new Bill Bryson or Irvine Welsh.

If you get really lucky, maybe some designer will come up with something as distinctive as the black and white jackets that mark out Iain Banks' books, or the equally trademark artwork that is featured on the novels of Louis de Bernieres, (created by Jeff Fisher and the Button Design Company).

In recent years, in an attempt to market books more successfully, there's been an interesting cloning of covers. Following the success of one book, **Memoirs of a Geisha**, for example, other, apparently similar titles will be packaged with very similar designs, a sort of suggestion to potential readers that, 'If you liked that, you'll probably enjoy this.'

We also saw it with the interchangeable covers of the 'chick-lit' genre of the late Nineties following in the wake of Helen Fielding's **Bridget Jones'** success, as a whole lot of other writers jumped on that particular bandwagon.

But as a midlist writer, with just a few thousand books being printed, you'd be wise to bide your time. Keep schtum and, unless your 1880s-set period novel actually features a car chase on the cover, agree with more or less anything.

Having said this, it was difficult for me to keep quiet when I saw the artwork for my first hardback. There was no hint of the book's menace, no suggestion of the darkness implied in the title.

I was delighted to be being published, but disappointed with the cover of this, my first book.

Tips and Summary:

If you make it this far, count your blessings that you are being published, and weep in private about the cover.

CWA

'I long ago came to the conclusion that all life is 6 to 5 against.'

Damon Runyon

The second thing my editor said to me – after she'd accepted my first book for publication – was that I should join the Crime Writers' Association. I'd never heard of this organisation but, had I given it any thought at all, I guess I could have imagined that there must be some loose affiliation of crime writers, just like there probably is for lighthouse keepers and dog-handlers.

After all, it's a lonely business up there, with just the word processor as company, for days, weeks at a time.

I sent my cheque for thirty-five quid. There were two rates, one for London members, and one for out-of-towners – I think they were called 'country members'. It was the first time I'd been glad to have an address in the sticks.

I received a white membership card with *CWA* printed on it in red, and a couple of crossed daggers as background.

As well as the membership card came the monthly crime writers' magazine, *Red Herrings*. The whole thing gave the appearance of having been dreamt up over a boozy lunch in the 1950s.

The CWA, it transpired, *had* been inaugurated by crime novelist, John Creasey and a few friends over a (boozy?) lunch in 1953.

At about the same time, **Night's Black Agents** was nominated for the Best First Crime Novel Award. I'm not sure that the two things were unconnected. My understanding was that you didn't, in fact, have to be a CWA member for your book to be nominated for that prize (or any other). But, a bit like those competitions on the back of cereal packets to win a car or a foreign holiday, and in which the small print is legally obliged to state that you do not have to even *buy* a packet of Cornflakes to enter, I rather doubt that the winner is ever anyone who has *not* invested in Mr Kellogg's breakfast product.

In any event, a member of the CWA or not, the author of **Night's Black Agents** did *not* win the Best First Crime Novel Award. And nor did anyone else: in 1993, for the first time in the Prize's history, none of the entries was adjudged good enough to win this award for a *first* novel.

One of the things that I immediately liked about being a member of the CWA, is that one is forbidden to pass on any of the information in *Red Herrings* to anyone who is *not* a CWA member. I had never been a member of a neo-secret society.

Trouble was, on reading the magazine, I couldn't imagine who it was you could pass on the information *to*. Who else was going to want to know about 'Chapter' lunches in St Albans, details of the next AGM, and news of members' forthcoming publications in large print editions?

But anyway, just to be on the safe side, I have always kept my own copies secure, don't read them on the train or in the pub, and keep my membership card out of sight, tucked away between my Sainsbury's Nectar card and my library issue ticket.

When I first joined, meetings were held once a month, with time off for summer holidays, the awards ceremonies in the autumn, and the Christmas party season. It was obviously quite a social whirl, and I wondered just when these crime writers did their writing, what with all the meetings, conferences and conventions.

No matter, notwithstanding the thinness of the card that vouchsafed my membership, the venue for London meetings was no less a place than the Groucho Club in London's Soho.

Bugger the thirty-five quid membership: this would show the folks back home. They might still be pulling down twenty-five grand a year teaching Dickens and Hardy, but, hey, I was a *writer*.

Not only did I earn fifteen hundred pounds for the eighteen months or so that it took me to write a novel, but I was now slumming it in the louche world of Groucho's, a place where writers, artists, media denizens and feisty stand-ups got drunk, cut deals, and probably did outrageous things in the lavatories.

I arrived early for my first meeting, approached the reception desk and, in a voice that trilled somewhat, asked for the CWA rooms. One of the leggy women in black who sat there pointed to the stairs.

As I passed it, I looked through to the bar. It was late afternoon and there was the hum and buzz that accompanies long drinking sessions. There was boozy laughter and fun in the air. The sort of laughter that puts Lady Dedlock 'quite out of temper' when she witnesses the happy scenes at the keeper's lodge at the beginning of Dickens' **Bleak House**.

I climbed the narrow staircase: first floor, second floor. I was feeling heady and short of breath and wondered whether it was Soho altitude sickness, or something more serious.

Outside a room on the third floor was a trestle table, the sort that decorators use when they are pasting wallpaper. I bought a glass of white wine from the woman standing behind it.

Inside the room, sitting on gilt-painted chairs with red padded seats were ten or fifteen people.

Apart from a tall man in dark glasses who was wearing a baseball cap, most of the people in the room appeared to be the wrong side of fifty.

I took a seat at the back of the room.

A man in a blue anorak who was carrying several carrier bags, opened one of them, pulled out a carefully wrapped cheese sandwich and started to eat it.

Eventually, the Chair introduced herself and the guest speaker, dealt with the minutes and declared the meeting open.

*

The couple of copies of *Red Herrings* that I had seen seemed to spend a deal of their pages devoted to the topic of just *where* CWA meetings should be held. Groucho's, it appeared, (even in a room on the vertiginous third floor) didn't want us to meet there any longer, and we were invited to offer suggestions about possible venues for the future.

Given that I was in a new romantic relationship, and relatively new to the capital, I was still making a timorous progress around London's dangerous streets, giving money to beggars on demand, and saying please and thank you when buying a paper or cigarettes. I didn't feel that I was going to be able to contribute much.

As well as the question of *where* meetings should be held, there was a more philosophical, ongoing debate about just *what* the CWA should be. The constitution stated, then as now, that the Association should be 'a non-political, non-sectarian body to promote the prestige and appreciation of crime writing.'

Apparently, some members felt that there was a need to enlarge this remit. There were pleas for wider membership, and suggestions that the CWA should be less exclusive, more open to ideas, for otherwise it was in danger of stultifying. There were some harsh statistics about the age of members, and a calculation that if new ones were not recruited soon, the time and venue for meetings would be irrelevant as most of the members would be unable to attend due to their having passed away.

This was not quite the heady stuff that I had hoped for, the cut and thrust of the writer's life: anecdotes, bookish gossip and tart barbs about wily agents and manipulative publishers.

It didn't help, either, that the tone of these remarks was often a little school-mistressy – a suggestion that if we didn't do something about things (such as attend monthly meetings – which, in fact, those of us in the room patently were doing anyway) and express views about the decisions being taken in our names, then our organisation would founder and crumble.

The trouble with this sort of hectoring appeal though, is that one never assumes that the remarks are directed at oneself. I sat through eight hours of the Live Aid concert, and was repeatedly harangued by Bob Geldof to send money. But it took all of those eight hours to finally realise that yes, he did actually mean *me*, and that it was *me* who was supposed to pick up the phone and send my tenner.

But in the case of the CWA, even if the dire warnings were true, I couldn't get over-excited about the possible collapse of something that I hadn't even known existed only a few months previously.

And anyway, I was a newly-published writer who lived most of the week in the provinces. What could I possibly contribute? I knew nothing about being a writer except that I had a book on the shelf that proclaimed that I now was one.

And, like a lot of folk who eventually get the break they've longed for, I secretly thought the whole thing was some kind of fluke or mistake, a sort of cosmic joke, the strings being pulled by a malevolent deity who would, at any moment now, boom out, 'Ha Ha, you've been had!'

After the guest speaker had talked for an hour about criminal law, I exchanged a few words with the person sitting next to me, and left.

It hadn't been quite the evening I'd anticipated.

As I stood in the foyer downstairs and waited for my girlfriend, MP and diarist Alan Clarke came in. He had a young woman on his arm, and he looked very happy. I felt even more like Lady Dedlock in **Bleak House**.

Since that evening in 1993, I've attended several London meetings in three or four different venues. There are also regional Chapter meetings, (a bit like Hell's Angels get-togethers, but with less leather and no Harleys). My local one's in Birmingham. We gather outside the library, and 'adjourn' to a nearby Italian restaurant for lunch. It's yet another variation on the London versus Regions theme that has exercised the minds of members for the last few years in a bid to find out how to keep the CWA vibrant.

The consensus was that those uppity Southerners expected us folks from sticksville to travel to the city just to get pushed around by a lot of insolent waiters in hotels, bars and clubs that didn't want us there anyway.

Ya boo and sucks to you, you lily-livered Londoners, seemed to be the message from the provinces, and so the current idea seems to be that committee members can get on their bikes, nip around the country and visit *us* at our regional Chapter lunches and breathe metropolitan life and blood into us.

I've stayed in the CWA for the last nine years, forking out my subscription each year to receive the monthly magazine, hear about other authors' publications, and posting details of my own. I've even contributed the odd piece about this or that, and witnessed the spats that sometimes go off between writers on touchy issues.

The CWA is also key in hosting things like the Dead on Deansgate crime writing festival in Manchester; the National Film Theatre's CrimeScene weekend, and compiling *The Times's* One Hundred Best Crime Novelists list.

In truth, my experiences with the Association have been mixed.

I've met some very nice people, and some of them have been very friendly and supportive through both good times and bad.

But, as with any group of people brought together who have one over-riding thing in common, writers are a mixed bunch, and it's not going to be easy to meld and blend them simply on account of their all following one trade or calling.

It's a difficult one to call. The CWA is run by, and for, its members, and if we don't submit stuff for the magazine, if we don't attend meetings and social events, the thing *will* wither. One recognises what a thankless task it is to organise these things.

And when there are mutterings of dissent, the understandable refrain is: if you don't like what's being done in your name, come and do better. Which, of course, I personally never do, because a) I'm not a committee man, and b) I find it hard enough to actually do my writing, read the odd book and the newspapers, watch the football on TV and have a pint, let alone organise events for fellow writers.

Of course, the CWA is only one of the many organisations where sad and lonely writers can feel close to other mortals. There's the Romantic Novelists' Association, The Society of Authors, and P.E.N. (the association for Poets, Playwrights, Editors, Essayists and Novelists where, a reliable source informs me, the wine is cheaper than at CWA functions, but the bitching tends to be even more ferocious).

Tips and Summary:

1) Don't do it

DEDICATIONS... AND FAMILY

In my father's house are many manuscripts...

I dedicated my first book to my mum and dad. I wasn't sure I had the wherewithal to write another, and I wanted to thank my mum for being the person who was responsible for my being a writer at all.

Mum was no more able to say 'Mr Ryan down the road bought a new car' than fly. It would be something like, 'Mr Ryan at number three, you know, they had the house painted last year, his wife was in hospital, they say it was varicose veins, but everyone knows what it was, well your father may not know, but he never knows anything. Anyway, Bill Ryan changed job and with the extra money, they were going to buy a caravan but Joan *hates* caravans, and so they got a new car.'

And so on. OK, it can you drive you mad – and sometimes *did* drive me mad – but I guess that Mum's inability to tell the most unremarkable tale without embellishment, editorialising and digressions, had its effect.

She couldn't walk to the shop or get on a bus without the whole thing being infused with interest, an interest beyond what was innately attached to the event, I suppose. And what is it that writers do? They live in the same world as everyone else, and similar things happen to them. They just imagine a little more, or connect disparate events, or describe the things that they are seeing with a little more colour and verve.

As well as being a storyteller, Mum was strong-willed and determined.

Dad was a much more easy-going and relaxed sort of person. He was from the south, from Sussex, my mum from Birmingham.

Anyway, they're my mum and dad and, as well as what Larkin

has to say about your parents, they were as good as they knew how to be.

While most writers choose to dedicate their novel to just one person (at the considerable risk of offending all the people that they have decided *not* to acknowledge) there is now also a fashion for multi-dedications, with endless thanks to myriad people.

The most gruesome that I have seen recently was Kathy Reichs's catchall dedication in her 2002 **Grave Secrets**: '*For the innocents: Guatemala 1962-1996. New York New York Arlington Virginia Shanksville Pennsylvania September 11 2001. I have touched their bones. I mourn for them.*' (Is there not something offensive about those personal pronouns, with their implication that Reichs's mourning is so much more heartfelt than anyone else's?)

Like speeches at the Oscars, I think a very little of this kind of thing goes a very long way.

When you've written as many novels as Reginald Hill, and you've already thanked friends, family, and trusted editors, you're down to the dog-sitters and the guy at the supermarket checkout, I guess. Hill dedicates **Arms and the Women** (2000) to '*Six proud walkers*', and then lists them all by name.

Ian Rankin introduced his 1997 CWA Gold Dagger winner **Black and Blue** without dedication, but with no fewer than *three* quotations – from James Ellroy; Robert Burns and Sydney Goodsir Smith:

'Weary with centuries
This empty capital snorts like a great beast
Caged in its sleep, dreaming of freedom
But with nae belief …'

But it's thriller writer, Dick Francis, who takes the royal biscuit. He dedicated his 2001 novel, **Shattered** '*To Her Majesty the Queen Mother on her 100th birthday...*' That'll take some beating.

Tips and Summary:

1) Keep dedications short
2) Keep quotations short, pithy and apposite

DISCIPLINE

'So, are you still working, or just doing the books?'
An old friend to Jack Higgins

One of the half a dozen questions that you are frequently asked as a writer is: How long does it take you to write a book? (Some of the others are: where do you get your ideas from? Do you have to be disciplined? How do you get an agent?)

How long *does* it take to write a book? Well, Georges Simenon used to write a novel in as little as two to three weeks. Prior to writing he'd have a medical examination and then sequester himself and write non-stop until the book was finished. His publishers must have loved him.

Either a strong creative urge made him work in this way or, possibly, the need to fund his affairs, wives and children: the Belgian-born author had a complex love life, with myriad lovers, wives and mistresses, and claims in his autobiography to have slept with thousands of women.

Another fecund author was founder of the Crime Writers' Association, John Creasey. The creator of the Inspector Gideon series of novels sometimes wrote his mysteries in little more than a couple of days.

Many writers relate how they have worked in similar periods of creative heat, fired with tremendous energy, their books written in intense bursts of work that almost defy belief.

But if that's how the book demands to be written, the need to create means that no amount of sleep deprivation, tetchiness, physical and mental punishment will stop an author who knows she/he is onto something.

Beryl Bainbridge (**Master Georgie,** 1998) is one writer who knows that these cauldron moments are not stress-free: 'When a book is nearing completion, I decide I've got to go to bed early so I can get up at five a.m. I drop off instantly, but then wake up at 11p.m., which is horrific. So I get up and try to write again. At two a.m. I look at what I've written and it doesn't make any sense, and so I put on the TV and watch a film. And then I'll go to bed, and get up at five a.m. At 8.30, I print off what I've done and then run around in circles wailing because it's so rubbish.'

Bainbridge is not alone in seeing in the dawn. Although there are exceptions, the vast majority of writers prefer to work in the morning, many of them in the very early morning.

Garrison Keillor (**Lake Wobegon Days**) likes to start as early as four or five a.m., 'with a sense of gratitude for the pure quiet'. Jeffrey Archer (**First Among Equals**) even prior to his recent imprisonment, would rise at five and be writing by six, continuing in two-hour blocks throughout the day, with two-hour breaks in between each session.

This enthusiasm to get on with the work is in marked contrast to popular perception and the oft-repeated clichés about writers confronting an intimidating blank page/screen. Margaret Forster (**Precious Lives,** 1998) says she cannot wait to get the top off her fountain pen each morning. And Rosalind Miles (**Guenevere: Queen of the Summer Country**) claims, 'I'm completely happy when I'm working – work is the only dignity.'

But it's not like this for everyone. Kingsley Amis used to feel extreme anxiety before getting down to work each morning. Bernice Reubens (**The Waiting Game,** 1997) keeps a piano and a cello in her study, and says that she'd 'rather do the ironing than start' but, 'If I write a good sentence, I give myself a little treat on the cello.'

Of course, not every writer feels the need to give himself to his work so exclusively. Many writers resent time away from their desks, but others manage to combine successful careers with significant output.

Philip Larkin ran the Hull University library for many years. TS Eliot worked for Lloyd's bank for nine years (at the same time as writing **The Waste Land**) before joining Faber and Gwyer (later to be Faber and Faber) as a literary adviser.

Many writers have found that they can combine teaching with writing. Theoretically, at least (although things have changed considerably during the last ten or twenty years), it's a conducive environment, with relatively short working days, longish holidays and a generally sympathetic milieu. David Lodge; Malcolm Bradbury; Anthony Burgess; DH Lawrence; TS Eliot and Gerard Manley Hopkins are just a few of the novelists/poets who have taught at some stage of their writing lives.

Andrew Davies, who has written plenty of original work, but is best known for his adaptations of the work of others for television (**Doctor Zhivago; Daniel Deronda; Pride and Prejudice; Vanity Fair** and **The Way We Live Now**) has said that he finds adapting classics for TV not dissimilar to teaching literature where, essentially, he would be saying to his students: 'Look at this book, isn't it wonderful.'

But the academic environment didn't suit Stephen King: '…for the first time in my life, the writing was hard. The problem was the teaching…I could see myself thirty years on wearing the same shabby tweed coats… in my desk drawer six or seven unfinished manuscripts…'

An early riser who successfully combined writing with the day job was Anthony Trollope. Up at five, he'd do his five hundred words, before setting about running the postal service. And, apparently, (though almost unbelievably, surely) he *meant* five hundred words.

Lots of writers leave the day's work at a point where they can pick up the baton and run with it, seamlessly, the following day. Margaret Forster goes so far as to stop at the foot of a page so that she doesn't have to read the previous day's work before beginning the next. But I find it hard to believe, as is said of Trollope, that he would literally stop in the middle of a sentence when his five hundred words were done. (Apart from anything else, who was counting!?)

For most of us, though, not able to inaugurate the collection of post through the use of red pillar boxes, travel all over Ireland on horseback, *and* rise at dawn to do five hundred words of a **Barchester Chronicle**, nor blessed with the fecundity of a Georges Simenon or John Creasey, our output is rather less impressive. But discipline is still the key. You may have the talent to write a novel '...*the boyish gift... to be plain and awkward...*' (WH Auden's **The Novelist**) but that talent will remain stillborn unless you combine it with the application required to stick at a piece of work that, for most mortals, usually takes about a year or so to complete.

But even though most of us can't produce a book in a couple of months, there's a lot to be said for getting the first draft out quickly. It's not at all unusual to be beset with doubts about just what it is you're doing.

If you can get your first draft down in a few weeks you are much less likely to be overwhelmed by, and give into, these doubts.

But perhaps you *should* have doubts: maybe the book doesn't have legs; maybe you are already losing your way, and the idea *does* need more thought and planning.

There are always lots of reasons for *not* writing a book, whereas there are very few for embarking on an undertaking that's going to be difficult, will make you miserable, tired, anti-social and generally unhappy. And that's only the *writing*.

But it's also true that if you wait too long, plan too long, make too many notes or talk too much about the book you are *going* to write, you'll probably never write it at all.

Writing a novel is (invariably) a private, a secret thing. As George Eliot has it in **Middlemarch**, 'We must keep the germinating grain away from the light.' It doesn't do to expose your fragile notions to the harsher elements of scrutiny too soon.

Starting is the hardest thing, but remember Susan Shaughnessy's advice: '*The writing you don't do today is lost for ever.*' It may sound a bit melodramatic, but there is some truth in it. TV writer Jim Hitchmough used to say, '*Don't get it right, get it written.*' And I've heard **Inspector Morse** creator, Colin Dexter, say that it doesn't matter how bad that first sentence is, get it down. If you've got it written, you can change it. Write a bad sentence, a terrible one, but get it written.

Only a few hours later, when you've worked on it and changed it and revised it and rejigged it, you might end up with something half decent that wouldn't otherwise have been done. It doesn't happen if you don't make that journey to your study and begin.

I'd had a few short stories and poems published when I began my first book, **Night's Black Agents.** I was lecturing full-time at a college of FE, and had a young family.

Sometimes, the last thing that I wanted to do (after the marking and preparation for the next day's teaching) was to go up to my writing shed and do another chapter on my book.

But I would still find the will to trudge up the garden path, switch on the word processor and work on my novel.

Something gets you going. I'm not sure what. Were we taken from the breast too soon? Ridiculed in the school playground? Not picked for the soccer team? I don't know. Is it the wish for recognition? A desire to join the ranks of those thousands of others who have done the same thing before us? Or is it simply some deeply-held wish to tell your story, to share your notions with others?

The thing that *keeps* you going is the fact that, in spite of all the setbacks, you have to believe that what you are doing is worthwhile: you are telling a story, and that story has 'legs'. It's big enough to sustain the length of a book – a minimum of some seventy thousand words.

Best of all, you have an idea, and ideas are very thin on the ground. When he was an elderly man, PG Wodehouse was asked why he no longer wrote short stories. 'If I get an idea these days, I make it last for a novel,' he replied candidly.

Lots of writers can pen a line. Journalists do it, short-story writers do it, people writing letters and emails do it. But to write a novel, to start, to plough on, to keep at it and maintain belief in it until it's finished, that's staying power.

Sadly, of course, it's also often insane, misguided and deluded. And there's the catch. Who's to say which it is that *you* are writing!

Unfortunately, to get your book written, let alone sold to a publisher, you're going to need huge reserves of inner strength and discipline, and a barrel of self-belief that borders on arrogance.

Try to write every day; if you don't, you'll lose the rhythm of your prose, as well as features of the plot, characters and, most importantly, your 'voice', the very timbre of the book that you are trying to maintain.

But even more important than these, if you don't write, you'll lose the habit. Now that's OK if you're *not* a writer; it'll be like forcing yourself to go to the gym. Everyone I know who has to *make* themselves go and work out gives it up in next to no time. I go to the squash court because I like playing squash. As long as the knees hold out, I'll be there. I often get beaten, and I get tired, but I love it.

If you really are a writer, you'll be like the person who plays squash or football because that's what he loves to do. Same with the writing: it's often hard, but it's often great too. It really is; it's about as good as it gets. David Beckham gets paid millions for playing for Manchester United. But if he got nothing at all, I can tell you, he'd *still* be playing football. Think of it that way. It's the only way to do it.

I write almost every day. Not only do I recognise the need for the discipline of doing it, but frankly, if I'm not writing, I don't feel 'whole'. To put it another way, I might be miserable when I'm doing it, but I'm *definitely* miserable when I'm not.

How often have I approached my work with trepidation, unsure of where I am going, lacking confidence in what has gone before, only to emerge from the study a few hours later with the smug tiredness that is one of the best sensations that I ever get: I've done a few pages more, completed a chapter, or begun a new one, like breaking new ground in the same way that you might turn the earth for spring planting. It's a very good feeling.

You need to have belief, and the best way of maintaining that belief is by driving through with the project. There will be all sorts of problems, all sorts of voices telling you not to go on. You are too tired; the idea is flawed and shallow; the prose is dead; the dialogue worse; there are too many books in the world already, and some of them are very, very good.

Everything's against you. Everything's telling you not to do it.

But if you're a writer, a real writer, i.e. someone who *writes*, you still do it. If you're lucky, the characters will start to live, the dialogue begin to spark and the prose sweeten.

When I'm writing a book, I'm like a dog with a bone. I have something that no one else has, and no one can take that something from me. It's a fine secret, and I'm driven. I write the first drafts in a gush. It's gobbledygook, and it flies onto the screen. If I'm writing longhand, it's illegible and unintelligible to anyone but me. There are deletions and arrows and asterisks all over the sheets; if it's on the screen, it's almost incomprehensible, with words that barely resemble the words that they are, so quickly are my fingers flying over the keyboard, my mind racing much faster than those fingers can keep up. It doesn't matter. It's exciting, and it's happening. Fifty, sixty, seventy per cent of it will never see the light of day. Most of it will end up in the bin or erased from the screen.

But it's there, it's a first draft, and without it, you have nothing. With it, like a chunk of undressed stone, I can work it. I can chip and hone and polish and reject and, at the end of it all, I'll have my book. It's long, it's quite ridiculously inefficient, and it's tiring, but it's also the only way that I have found that I can do it. And that's why that first draft, for me, for most of us, whether we're the fliers or the page-a-day creepers, is so important.

So: How long does it take to write a book? Well, the first one took me forty years. It might sound facetious, but in a way, it's true. That first book gathers into it so much that has been mulling and accruing for all of those years that who's to say *what* has gone into it?

Since then, they've been a deal quicker. If things go well, they take me only about a year now.

Tips and summary:

1) Don't talk it, write it.
2) Get *something* down. You can change it/scrap it later, but get something on the screen/page.
3) Try and write every day; be regular, it'll pay dividends.

DISTRIBUTION

'Greet press at market maketh dere ware,
And too greet chepe is holden at litel pris.'
Geoffrey Chaucer *The Wife of Bath's Prologue*

Distribution is key: if your book's not on the shelf who, apart from your dearest friends, your closest family, is going to be bothered to actually *order* a copy?

But retailers are reluctant to stock books that are not being heavily promoted, unless they are by authors with an appreciable following, and with sales to match, (and are therefore being heavily promoted!)

Of course, every writer wants his or her book to be in WH Smith and Waterstone's but, notwithstanding the 100,000-plus books published in the UK each year (a market that has grown by 6% since 2,000, and is reckoned to be worth some two and a half *billion* pounds per annum) if you are a 'midlist' writer, the reality is that you are unlikely to be one of them.

The decision about which books go into Smith's stores (nation-wide, as opposed to any deal that you are able to personally arrange with your local store) is made by a committee which meets at their head office in Swindon. But just how they choose *what* they choose, apart from the obvious bestsellers, is something of a mystery.

WH Smith has over five hundred shops and bookstalls across Britain, and sells more books than any of its rivals (including Waterstone's, who have 19% of the books market, compared with WH Smith's 22%). This might seem odd for a retailer that is not even a dedicated bookseller, but the fact is that Smith's are often selling books along with greetings cards and stationery in towns that do not support a dedicated bookshop.

With this many outlets, the books that the Swindon Smith's committee chooses to promote in any one month will put on phenomenal sales and guarantee them success as bestsellers.

In choosing these books, Smith's drives a very hard bargain on the publishers' price. There have also been mutterings in the book trade about publishers being forced to meet the promotional costs (advertising and window displays) of the retailer. But sales are so big that whether it's a three-for-two sticker on the flyleaf of the book (ironically, something which many readers, apparently, associate with the books being inferior, rather than their merely being heavily promoted) or a title being heavily discounted, publishers are delighted when it is one of their authors who is chosen for promotion by Smith's.

But even High Street locations aren't going to persuade the four out of five people in Britain who never go into a bookshop to start buying books. Recognising this fact, fourteen years ago, ex-policeman Ted Smart, and unemployed Seni Glaister, set up The Book People. Their direct bookselling business now has a turnover of one hundred million pounds a year.

It's still the case that a third of men didn't read a single book last year, and another third read fewer than five books in the same period, but The Book People, with their ploy of delivering a dozen titles to factories, offices, and school staff-rooms, and then returning in a fortnight's time to collect the orders, has been a phenomenal success.

And, of course, because of the volume of books sold in this way (they also do mail order and internet selling) they are able to order huge quantities of books and pay publishers (who in turn pay their authors) a fraction of what they would normally receive.

Although many other retailers, from supermarket outlets to the big book chains, are less than happy about the very big discounts that The Book People demand – and get – the thinking behind the operation is that these are books that are going to readers who often would not, otherwise, be buying at all. It's a new market that has been accessed.

In any event, if readers can buy Alan Titchmarsh's book on gardening for £6.99, rather than £18.99, or the *complete* Booker Prize shortlist of six novels, (retail: £58.92) for a laughable £9.99, they are going to attract buyers, that's for sure.

No wonder they were able to order 600,000 of Jamie Oliver's first **Naked Chef,** something for which, apparently, he came and thanked the sales reps personally. He saw it as the thing that broke him through to his television career and everything that has followed.

This remarkably simple operation, with an army of reps on the road delivering to some 30,000 shops, offices and factories, now sells some 14 *million* books per year to two and a half million customers.

Because they place only firm orders, (i.e. none of their ordered stock can be returned to the publishers if they make a buying error) they need to be fairly cautious about what they take on. But they do sometimes go out on a limb with a title. It was The Book People who, a decade ago, ordered – and sold – 600,000 hardback copies of the Yorkshire daleswoman, Hannah Hauxwell's memoirs, **Daughter of the Dales** and **Seasons of my Life.**

Having said this, I wouldn't put money on them opting for a title by a midlist writer, something which would send the author into the bestseller list, and make his bank manager happy, even if he was only collecting a fraction of the royalty that he would normally expect from his publisher.

There is, though, a rather better chance of the midlist writer finding himself in the catalogue of one of the conventional book clubs. They sell mail order, but require buyers to take a minimum number of books per year in return for heavily subsidised opening offers. Books are offered for as little as a penny each as a come-on, and subsequent titles are attractively priced.

The whole point of the operation is to sell big quantities of popular titles, but some of them, QPD in particular, *do* sometimes back a midlist title that they think might have appeal. But mostly, it's Catch 22: when you're famous, your titles will feature. You can then sell more books, and be more famous.

It's said that the very best recommendation, whether it's for a restaurant, a film, play or book, is still word of mouth. And while it's true that a few words between trusted friends and readers is never going to lead to the sort of sales that direct selling and heavy discounting of popular titles does, people who discover books in this way tend to be passionate in their advocacy of them.

And then, if the author is fortunate, word gets around amongst readers, and the publisher's home and dry. It certainly happened with both Frank McCourt's **Angela's Ashes** (1996)and Louis de Bernieres's **Captain Corelli's Mandolin** (1994), whose proselytising readers made them cult reads before they became bestsellers.

Advertisements, especially in London, where there are significantly higher numbers of readers than elsewhere (particularly on the tube) obviously have some power to influence choice. OK, I know that many of those readers on the Piccadilly Line are clutching their book in an attempt to ward off the attentions of the mad person sitting across the aisle from them, but many of them (especially women; men appear to prefer newspapers) *are* actually reading books, and this is a very big market.

As a midlist writer, assuming that the direct sellers or book clubs don't swoop on your titles and make you famous, (unlikely) if not exactly rich (*highly* unlikely) and even if you are lucky enough to get your titles onto the shelves of the major bookshop chains, what else is required for them to move? Will they sell, or will they simply sit there for a couple of months, before being returned to the publisher?

Covers are obviously important, and so is 'blurb', the outline of the book's contents printed on the back cover (and often written by the author himself).

But it is the browsing that fascinates me. I've watched people come into bookshops and browse. I've also sat behind tables at book-signing sessions — sometimes alone, sometimes with other writers — and I've watched as readers pick up books and 'browse' them. What exactly are they looking for? They glance at the cover; they look at the blurb. They then flip through the book, stop at a page, and they read a line or two. (This seems to be the case whether they are doing it self-consciously, with the writer sitting in front of them, or unobserved.)

When they return the book to its place, or actually decide to buy it, I have often wanted to ask them just what it was they were *looking* for. Which magical words, exactly, would prompt them to think, Yes, I'll take this? (Or, indeed, the opposite?)

The blurb on my crime novels is interesting enough, I think. The reviews, either selected from previous titles, or taken from the hardback editions for the paperback, could really hardly be better. So just what is it that a potential purchaser needs to see that will make him actually buy the book?

Truth to tell, I've absolutely no idea.

But then again, the very idea of 'browsing' for a book has always struck me as a wonderfully undirected, almost indolent, pastime. I'm not knocking it, the contrary: I rather wish I could do it. Unfortunately, when I go into a bookshop, I already have a mental list of at least half a dozen titles that I'm looking out for, or will recognise as soon as I see them, either from reviews I've read in the broadsheets, or from the recommendations of friends.

'Browsing', simply idling along the shelves and stacked tables, and stumbling upon this or that novel or biography that I've never heard of, would be a real pleasure. It just never happens. The idea of picking up something I've never heard of, and buying that, rather than one of the several books that I know I *should* read, (and indeed, probably *want* to read) is almost unthinkable.

When someone tells me about a book that they're enjoying, I always ask them how they came to be reading it. The answer, frequently, is that they 'just saw it in the bookshop and it looked good'. What freedom. What liberated, unstructured reading. How I envy them.

Tips and Summary:

1) If you're a midlist writer, get a job working in a Waterstone's, WH Smith or Book People store/warehouse. It's almost certainly the only way these companies will be featuring your name.

EDITORS

'A good many young writers make the mistake of enclosing a stamped, self-addressed envelope, big enough for the manuscript to come back in. This is too much of a temptation for the editor.'

Ring Lardner

I dedicated my third novel, **Until Dawn Tomorrow**, to Elizabeth Walter, my original editor at Collins. Without her I could, quite possibly, have been submitting my work to agents and publishers to this day.

To be a published writer, you need a little bit of talent, a lot of determination and a chunk of luck but, at the end of the day, someone, somewhere, has got to believe in your work.

For me, that person was Elizabeth. She had been crime fiction editor at HarperCollins for many years when she accepted for publication my first book. She retired in 1994, a year after she had decided to publish **Night's Black Agents**.

Of course, it's true, a publisher's reader, someone whom I will never know, and whom I never met, first selected my book from the slush pile to go forward to Elizabeth. And there were, no doubt, others involved in that decision-making process, but it was *she* who got behind the book and made sure that I was published. I am only one of many, many authors that Elizabeth Walter assisted into print.

While **Night's Black Agents** had been being repeatedly rejected the previous year, largely to try and keep sane, I had started work on a second book. **Less Than Kind** was accepted by Elizabeth just a few months after publication of the first book, but seen through to publication by Julia Wisdom, her successor at HarperCollins.

When the first novel was eventually published, therefore, I'd already done several months' work on **Less Than Kind**. I only hoped that my publisher didn't think that I could continue to turn out books at this (apparent) rate of one every few months!

After Elizabeth's retirement, and Julia's move across from Gollancz to occupy her predecessor's chair, I enjoyed a (relatively) halcyon period of success. **Night's Black Agents** was nominated for the CWA John Creasey Best First Crime Novel Award; **Less Than Kind** was published in hardback, and both titles were sold to a large print publisher.

As a bonus, whereas Elizabeth had told me when she bought the first book that it was highly unlikely that I would go into paperback until I had at least *three* titles to my name, Julia's first act was to publish paperback editions of the first two titles.

The graphics department came up with decent artwork for the covers: moody and atmospheric for **Night's Black Agents**; hip and fittingly seedy for **Less Than Kind**.

Julia also took the radical step of dropping the word '*Club*' from the Collins Crime list. Formerly published as Collins Crime *Club*, by the 1990's this umbrella title sounded a bit passé, and made the books published under its imprint sound as if they were part of some coterie group, but a group whose exclusivity was of exactly the *wrong* sort, as if readers of them were subscribing to *Chiropody Monthly*, or some such.

In 1995, I asked Elizabeth if I might dedicate my third book, **Until Dawn Tomorrow** to her, and she graciously accepted.

Not long before the book was due to go to press, some minor editorial changes were required. Deadlines were tight, and I was invited to make the amendments at HarperCollins offices in Fulham Palace Road.

After talking through a few points in Julia's office, I sat at a desk in an adjoining office with my manuscript and pencil.

I'm in Rupert Murdoch's swanky building in west London. There are water coolers and tropical plants. Young women float about the place to a quiet background of office murmur. They take calls and send faxes as I make the final corrections to my book, a book that HarperCollins appear keen to publish.

You might want to turn out for England at Wembley, or score a hundred at Old Trafford. For me, it doesn't get much better than this.

Only five years later, Julia wrote to my agent, to tell her that it was with regret that they (HarperCollins) were not going to publish my latest book, **Small Vices**.

A few months previously, I had written to tell her that I'd restarted the book, and that after a difficult period, things were now going well (a part truth: the book was underway, and I had a general notion of where it might go, but there was a lot to do, a lot to work out. For no matter how much I try to plan, I find I can only write a book by *writing* it. It's the excitement, it's the buzz, but it's also very long-winded, draft after draft after draft).

She wrote back to say that she was delighted that the book was coming along well but, given the long 'lead-in' times, and the need to print next year's catalogue, would I send her what I'd done so far.

Oh, dear. I *never* show work in progress. That's what it is: work in progress.

But she was very persuasive. And, of course, you always have a sneaking suspicion that what you've done/are doing is really pretty good.

She insisted that she would not be influenced by what she saw, she just needed to get a 'flavour' of the book. But can anyone dismiss first impressions? Of a book? A person? A car?

I sent her the first dozen chapters of **Small Vices.**

She wrote back: she liked what she had read. Yes, really, she did.

But what she was looking for from me was a 'bigger book'. (My first novel had been a mere hundred and eighty pages, but since then they had been putting on weight of about twenty pages per title, and the last one had come in at close to two hundred and forty.)

She explained that she did not mean 'bigger' in the sense of another thirty pages; what she meant was a book with a bigger *theme*, a wider *canvas*. Trouble is, this is not the kind of book I write. I can no more do 'big' than Anita Brookner can do James Herbert.

No matter, I ploughed on, and did my best to make **Small Vices** 'bigger'.

Six months later, after endless revisions, I sent one copy to my agent, and one to Julia at HarperCollins.

My agent phoned to say that she was delighted with the book.

As the weeks passed though, the silence from the HarperCollins building in Fulham Palace Road felt ominous.

My agent assured me that all would be well: *we* both knew that **Small Vices** was the best book that I had written.

After several months, Julia faxed my agent. She likes the book very much; she feels that it is the best novel that I have written. (I like the book; my agent likes the book; now my editor, too, likes the book. This is *good*.)

However... (always the *However*...) unfortunately, she does not feel that **Small Vices** is going to 'break me out of' my current position. And, with Rupert Murdoch's accountants scrutinising every author's sales, 'It is with very much regret that HarperCollins cannot...' etc. etc.

I'd read the runes, of course, seen the little signs and picked up the whispers and bits of body language, so it was no great surprise. And the publishing world was rife with stories of 'culls' of midlist writers.

My reviews had been excellent, but with four titles published, I had not become a household name. Perhaps a bit of publicity and advertising might have helped? Quite how the breakthrough was expected to occur without these is something of a mystery.

A few days later my agent sent a very nice note in which she suggested that this might be a good time for us to 'make a fresh start'.

I now not only had no publisher, I had no agent either.

Strangely, and to my complete surprise, as well as feeling the hurt and sadness of rejection, I also felt some relief. For a *very* brief period, I felt unburdened. Perhaps I no longer *had* to be a writer?

To be free of that self-imposed burden of the daily grind. The discipline, the thankless toil, the constant anxiety. And the waiting, always the waiting: to finish this chapter, that book, get it copy-edited, get it published, await the reviews. And then to begin the whole cycle again. Always the waiting, never arriving, never finished.

(And, of course, like all paranoid people, even if the price *is* great, to have one's suspicions confirmed is reassuring for those of us who almost value being right above being happy!)

But that sense of relief did not last long, and within a week, I was putting together my publishing CV, a selection of my reviews and book jackets, and posting them off to agents and editors. Yet again.

I wrote to a big publisher whose crime editor I knew slightly. Things looked very promising for a couple of weeks while she investigated the possibility of selling my books in America.

The prospect of being sold in America is second only to the joyous notion of getting one's books adapted for television. The bad news, though, is that I know that my books are very *English*. London, Manchester, Birmingham and the Welsh Borders are their milieu. What will the citizens of Ohio and Arkansas, New York and Carmel make of tales and people set in these places?

Nothing, it seems. She wrote to tell me that the books are too

English to make much impression in America. She very much regrets, etc. etc.

It was the same with a couple of hot-shot agencies. They love my writing, and are certain that I will find a publisher for my new book, but it is with regret that...

It was like the old days, working my way through **The Writers' and Artists' Yearbook.** Just a bit worse, perhaps.

Listening to Radio Four's *Front Row* one evening about *Sunday Times* journalist Paul Eddy's one million pound deal for his new thriller, **Flint,** I was pricked into emailing Mark Lawson to say that most writers inhabit a very different world from Paul Eddy's.

A week later, in a live edition of the programme, John Mitchinson, head of Cassells, Mark Lawson and myself discussed the plight of the 'midlist' writer.

A week after the programme went out, I signed a deal with Allison & Busby, a south London-based publisher with a good list.

I was back in the team.

Small Vices was published in November 2001. The *Literary Review* called it 'brilliantly written, implacably argued ...' and claimed that it set 'a dazzling standard for the year.'

Tips and Summary:

1) Don't be a writer
2) Be nice to your editor
3) Meet your deadline and accept editorial advice
4) Try not to weep in public when your publisher drops you

EPIPHANY

'It may be true that the real writer writes, but most people believe that a real writer is one who is **published***.'*

Anon

In the days before email, I became expert at reading my mail. From the outside. Those days of waiting for important news in a letter seem quaint now, but I was often up at seven-thirty, peering up and down the road looking for the postman.

He'd park his red bike in my opposite neighbour's drive and disappear up the road with his sack. I'd make some coffee and then hear the clunk and thud of my flap and the mail tumble (several letters) or waft (a dull circular or home-loan offer) to the hall floor.

The kind of letter that I wanted was in a white A5 envelope. The envelope would be thick, woven paper, and it would have come first class.

I'd read the postmark and decipher exactly *where* in London (it had to be London, of course) it had been posted.

The best letter I was likely to receive (feedback, a foreign sale, or an acceptance/offer on the new book) would be from my publisher (Hammersmith), or my agent (Shepherd's Bush).

The second best letter would be a cheque (royalty; advance, or on publication).

The third best would be a love letter. (I often thought that the ideal would be to have a love affair *with* your agent.)

JK Rowling has written about getting 'the' telephone call and standing on the stairs in a state of shock.

Stephen King knew there was something wrong when he was summoned to the phone while teaching a literature class in Hampden High School in the USA. He picked up the receiver to be told that Doubleday had bought his first novel, **Carrie.**

My favourite story, though, concerns family barrister and crime novelist Elizabeth Woodcraft. Elizabeth was a member of the London University creative writing group, CityLit.

One evening, literary agent Annette Green came along to the group. Elizabeth asked whether she might send the agent her novel, **Good Bad Woman.**

Two days later Ms Green phoned. Apparently, she actually used the words, 'I couldn't put it down.'

Elizabeth is now on her third book for HarperCollins in a series featuring Motown-music-loving, family barrister Frankie Richmond.

These are heart-warming stories, of course, but sadly, for most of us, by the time we actually get the letter, the telephone call, the e-mail or fax, we'll have already tried to top ourselves several times, and any joy that we might otherwise feel will be tinged with pain, dulled by Prozac and booze, and the broken spirit that we are nursing.

Worn down by the struggle and pain of getting our book into print, we've little appetite for celebration when (if) that moment arrives.

In 1989, Samuel Johnson's cathedral city was inviting submissions for The Lichfield Prize. And what a prize it was: £5,000 *plus* guaranteed publication of the winning entry.

To qualify, one's book had to be unpublished, and it had to be set in 'the Lichfield area'. Unfortunately, the book I was writing, **Night's Black Agents,** was set in Birmingham and the North West.

I spent half-term in Staffordshire rewriting the book, trying to overcome bridges and tunnels being in the wrong place, distances between places being awry, there being a town where I needed the anonymity of a city, and villages popping up where I needed a deserted towpath for a quiet murder.

A month later my entry was in. Two months later and the judges wrote that my book was on the shortlist of six.

In his speech, one balmy July evening, chair of the judges, crime novelist HRF Keating, touched on the strengths of each of the half dozen short-listed books. Listening to his few words about **Night's Black Agents** was like watching a dear friend disappear over the horizon.

Keating announced that radio journalist Val Kershaw's novel, **Rock-a-Die Baby** was the winner. We filed up to 'congratulate' her.

The drive back home to Shropshire was long and mournful.

As a writer, you work alone, drop out of circulation for long periods when the work's intense, and you're frequently anti-social. I've often met people on the street three months after I last saw them, and they look at me as much as to say: 'Oh, you're still alive, then?'

When BT asked me to choose a number for my 'Best Friend' so that I could get 20% off the calls to that number, my Best Friend was the local leisure centre where I play squash a couple of times a week!

When that first book was eventually taken, there was no euphoric phone call, just a warm letter from Collins expressing interest. This was followed by another, then there was a phone call, and eventually, lunch.

But even then, I couldn't celebrate. My (original) manuscript was still with the independent publisher who, despite my having signed a contract with him, and his repeated claims that he was going to publish the book, had not done a thing with it for the many months that he had sat on it in his 'office' in Great Eastern Street.

Now, with an offer from a bona-fide publisher, I had to undertake the delicate task of retrieving the manuscript from him. This necessitated my hanging around an East End tube station for two hours one Sunday morning waiting for a publisher/businessman who didn't arrive.

At last, just about to leave and rue my ill-luck, he hoved into view, manuscript in his hand.

A week later, with his signed disclaimer in my possession, I was able to sign my contract with HarperCollins.

Like everything else in this wretched business, for most of us, there's no moment of epiphany. It's the slog and the pitch, the follow-up phone calls and letters, the excuses and rejections and waiting, and then, fools that we are, we start the whole miserable business over again.

So why *do* we do it?

Well, for all the frustration and heartache, the knocks and disappointments, there is some solace.

There's no fame, no glory and very little money, but if you're a writer, there *is* the quiet satisfaction of sitting on a train, in the cinema, or with chums in the pub, and just knowing: Hey, I'm a writer.

Tips and Summary:

1) Don't do it.
2) Don't hold your breath for the big moment. By the time it comes, you'll have expired.

FESTIVALS

'Thanne longen folke to goon on pilgrimages...'
Geoffrey Chaucer *The Canterbury Tales*

'Festival' is an odd word for such a widespread cause of misery, a bit like using 'holiday' as a synonym for 'illness'.

Hay on Wye, Winchester, Brighton, Cheltenham. Even Shrewsbury had a literature festival last year. In the current **Writers' and Artists' Year Book**, fifty-one festivals are listed, from Hay and Bath to the less likely Ilkley and Leicester. And these are merely the ones that are cited from the hundreds – 'too many to mention,' says the book – that are actually staged. The heart plummets.

I was invited to Shrewsbury's inaugural event. It wasn't Hay, exactly, but it was OK. I did a little talk and workshop on a rainy Sunday afternoon in one of the annexes to the library. There were half a dozen of us: a couple of very nice Americans, a librarian from the Shropshire town, another local lady, and an archivist. I'd prepared some writing exercises, did a couple of readings and we had a question and answer session at the end.

A couple of the people there had attended lots of the events that weekend, and they might well have been expected to be suffering from festival fatigue. But they said that they had enjoyed their Sunday afternoon gig with me as much as anything. They didn't *have* to say that.

During the last few years, I've been to quite a few festivals, but the first big one was in 1998. The Crime Writers' Association, in conjunction with Waterstone's, keen to promote the genre and its practitioners, staged Dead on Deansgate – in Manchester.

Hard-boiled and cosy; noir and gay; American and British; procedural and forensic; serial and comic; non-fiction and 'true', we'd all be there.

111

Hard-pressed, unpaid committee members, in conjunction with the booksellers, spent months planning the event in the happening north western city.

As requested, I submitted my biography and photo, and made myself available for this and that panel – forums at which authors would talk about selected topics to fans.

There would be a drinks reception to open the event, lots of readings and social events, a jazz combo led by crime writer John Harvey, the whole rounded off with a gala dinner at the Ramada hotel at the end of Deansgate.

On the first day, I trudged through the rain from St Peter's Square down to Deansgate.

Waterstone's windows were full of crime novels. There were dozens of books there. One writer had *four* of her titles on display there. There were none of mine.

I made my way down to The Ramada, the city-centre hotel that was the joint centre of the operation. At two o'clock, the first panel of the afternoon was due to begin. We were due on at three.

The two o'clockers were drafting in substitutes: the London train had been delayed with half the participants on it. When I looked through the doors of the Carroll Suite, I could see that there were sixty or seventy people there. I had been expecting a dozen.

The panel got underway as girls from Waterstone's arranged piles of books on the baize-covered tables in the first floor foyer.

At a quarter to three, a woman bustled in, dropped her coat on the floor, handed her luggage trolley to someone, and sailed through the doors muttering something about the London train. A second later there was a tide of applause from within.

No time had been allotted for change-over at the end of one panel and the start of the next one, or for getting in and out of the suite to do book signings and so, at three o'clock, as people tried to talk to authors at the front of the room, they were unceremoniously ushered out as we, the next panel, assumed our positions.

There were radio microphones on each of the big, easy chairs. The Perrier bottles were empty, the glasses smeared. People trickled in. Our moderator, Gemma O'Connor (**Farewell to the Flesh,** 1998) wanted to start, but it was barely three and I urged her to wait. The room gradually filled.

As Gemma introduced us, I wondered whether the microphone was picking up my irregular breathing. I wasn't particularly nervous; it is, after all, about the only thing I think I know about.

But, of course, it's easy to look around the room, stop listening, get distracted, and then have no idea what the question is that is being shunted around between us. Which is exactly what happened.

Caught in a daze and invited to speak, I'm surprised by the amplified sound of my own voice around the room. I do rapid delivery. And, because I lack confidence in the merit of what I have to say, I make not very witty remarks, and employ a deal of transparently false modesty.

Our panel's theme is 'the importance of location'. What I appear to be saying is something about the importance of feelings and relationships, *irrespective* of time or place. For some unaccountable reason, I'm citing **Antony and Cleopatra.**

Gemma intervenes with a remark about Helen Mirren as Cleopatra 'getting her kit off'.

It trolls along for a bit. Nothing particularly awkward or sticky, but nothing riveting either.

At question time, it becomes dispiritingly clear that the entire audience is made up of *other* writers. Where are the fabled fans? The crazed readers? The stalking devotees of the genre who are going to want to buy books and have the secrets of our calling revealed to them?

When I get out to the foyer, the other panellists are already in their places, and wielding pens in the pose more beloved of most writers than actually writing books.

I take my seat, and eventually a nice woman with an armful of novels asks me to recommend one of the books that I have brought along. I feel like a waiter recommending dishes on a restaurant menu and sign a copy of **Thought For The Day** ('Unequivocally excellent,' *Sunday Times*) for her.

Two hours. One panel. One paperback sale. Spirits … lowish.

I wander back up Deansgate to Waterstone's to catch the second half of Nicholas Blincoe answering questions about his work. He's young(ish), sharp-suited, and has an engaging manner. He looks like he's in the here and now, and he's 'hot' right now, with a couple of well-received novels (**Manchester Slingback,** 1998, and **Jello Salad,** 1997).

At five, I head for the public library where HRF Keating opens the *Blood on the Streets* exhibition. Keating makes a plea for the crime genre, commends the libraries for their support, and thanks Manchester writers for their endeavours in orchestrating this event.

There are A4 folded leaflets with details of we writers from each sub-genre represented on them. I go from one pile to the next. I know I'm not an American, and that my books don't feature a female private eye, but I'm eventually reduced to looking even here as, sadly, the information about *this* author is nowhere to be found.

I'm not going to cry, but I am sad. Why have I been asked to submit a biography and photograph, and yet nothing has been used? I might as well not be here. I have told friends and family about this event, and some of them may even come, but they will find no mention of the writer who has invited them. Is there a conspiracy?

I slope around the corner to the Lord Mayor's Civic Reception. The first good news of the day: we are allowed to *smoke*. I roll a Golden Virginia.

The Mayor's a jovial chap who, for the first ten minutes gives no indication of knowing why we writers are here. Or maybe he just gives his 'Manchester's a wonderful city...' puff to all-comers, and simply amends the last five minutes of his speech according to his audience?

We get a history lesson on the cotton city, and then a deal on the City Hall in particular, right down to its 'sixteen fireplaces' and how the original architect won the commission.

He eventually mentions that his wife is a crime reader (this is familiar stuff: 'I don't actually read it myself, but I know someone who does').

He goes on to tell us that, although our convention is called *Dead on Deansgate,* no one's murdered on the main street nowadays, as Manchester is a 'twenty-four hour city with nightlife the equal of London, and better than Paris'.

I think he should get out more.

Manchester resident, Val McDermid, responds to the Mayor's welcome, telling us how much she loves the city and that she will never leave it. We are then free to wander around and look at the sixteen fireplaces, high ceilings and the many paintings of cotton endeavour in the nineteenth century.

Rather lowered by my day as a crime writing delegate at one of the biggest conventions of its kind ever held in Britain, I head back to the Metro in the wind and rain.

But, as my mother often said, Hope springs eternal. The next day, I decide to catch crime novelist Susan Moody, talking to Morse-man, Colin Dexter.

Dexter is amusing and erudite. He has advice for would-be writers in the audience, and a couple of funny anecdotes, even if they are a little hoary and burnished through use. 'The beginning is one half of the deed,' he says. 'Forget the muse, forget best first sentence; write the *worst* first sentence, and then improve it.'

He's generous in acknowledging that the casting of John Thaw as Morse was critical to the success of the TV series.

(A few years previously, when I happened to be introduced to Anthony Minghella (*Truly, Madly, Deeply; The English Patient*) the film director told me that he very nearly declined the job of writing the screenplay for the first TV Inspector Morse.)

Dexter winds up by telling us that, a bit like Hitchcock's cameo appearances in his own films, he (Dexter) was sometimes given tiny parts in the Morse films. Dressed as a bishop, and having lunch in a local pub with the crew during a break in filming, someone approached him with the words, 'Excuse me, your Grace...'

He even made the on-screen credits on the fifth series, being described as, 'Second dog handler'. There was no dog in the film, he confides!

I'm keen to hear about small publishing houses (I suspect that I might be looking for one if HarperCollins don't care for my new book), but I also want to sit in on Natasha Cooper's panel on Child Abuse in Fiction.

I get thirty minutes of each before hurrying back to Waterstone's.

The convention programme has finally arrived. After the disappointment of yesterday's Waterstone's window (no books) and the Lord Mayor's reception (no author pamphlet) it's a relief to see my mug and biography there.

I listen to a few words from each of the nominees for *this* year's John Creasey Prize for Best First Crime Novel. I'm pleased for the recipients, but am always minded that there is no second chance for a *first* novel prize. It still rankles.

Writer Minette Walters, agent Lisanne Radice, and editor Maria Rejt discuss the evolution of a novel. Although she's hugely successful, Minette hasn't forgotten the hunger, the dedication, joys and tears that get a book written, revised, and eventually taken.

Surprisingly, what none of the panellists acknowledge is the one thing that no writer can do without: a bit of luck.

You have to be able to write, you have to be able to give old ideas new spin, dream up new situations and characters, but most of us who can do these things could just as easily remain unpublished: you have to be *lucky*, too.

That evening, at the gala dinner, I sit next to a Finnish novelist and the crime fiction editor of Constable. We chat and drink happily through the three courses. My editor is on the top table with guest of honour, American writer, Jeffery Deaver (**The Coffin Dancer,** 1998).

After the presentation and the speeches, I sidle up to her for a few words. Do I sense just a little 'distance', a hint of reserve? She's had a few chapters of **Small Vices** for some weeks now. Does she hate it, or am I being paranoid?

Tips and Summary:

1) Don't do it, it's bad for your health and digestion

GETTING CLOSE ... BUBBLING UNDER

'Writing a first novel takes so much effort, with such little promise of result or reward, that it must necessarily be a labour of love bordering on madness.'

Steven Saylor

In April 1992, I took my A-level literature students to Wellington College for the day.

There were no crime novels on our syllabus amongst the Trollope and Hopkins and Shakespeare, but writers Susan Moody and Simon Brett were giving a workshop about detective fiction.

All my adult life, I've liked the idea of writers and writing. At twenty, before I'd been to university, before I'd even gone back to college to get some 'O' and 'A' levels to *go* to university, I remember spending hours typing up Dylan Thomas's letters from one of the Sunday broadsheets. No more, no less, just typing columns of newspaper print from the pages of the *Observer* onto a sheet of A4. It was a sort of unfocused homage, I suppose.

For some people it's soap stars or footballers, for me, it's writers.

So there we were, my A-level students and me, heading for Wellington. If my students wondered what we were doing in the mini-bus tootling down the A5, no one said.

After the talks and question and answer session, I approached Simon Brett for a quiet word. I've been published myself for a few years now, and I've given a few talks and workshops, so I know all about would-be authors wanting 'a word'.

I told Simon that I had recently finished my first book, was sending it out and that, although it was coming back to me, the rejections were encouraging.

I probably asked him for advice as to where else I might send my book. I don't remember his answer. But I do remember very well the encouraging phrase he used. He said, 'It sounds to me as if you're just bubbling under'. There was something about those few words that I remembered for years.

I next met Simon about five years later at a crime writers' meeting at the New Cavendish Club off Berkeley Square. I had just been fleeced at a mock auction on Oxford Street on my way there. (I wrote up the experience and pitched it to the *Evening Standard* as a feature. I lost a tenner and some pride at the 'auction', but I got £750 for my story and a double page spread in the paper the next evening.)

My first two books had been published and the third was due out shortly. I reminded Simon of our Wellington meeting. I told him I'd often thought about his comment that I was 'bubbling under', and the way it had somehow given me encouragement.

We've met several times since then. He's always been friendly and, on a couple of occasions, I've asked him for advice. (As well as a prolific novelist – the Charles Paris and Miss Pargeter books – Simon's a radio producer and TV and radio playwright.)

I mention this because if you do, foolishly, decide to try and make the parlous journey into print, I hope you have the good fortune to meet people as helpful and supportive as Simon has been to me.

If you want to be a writer, if perhaps you're 'bubbling under', you should do three things: read a lot, write a lot, and be a groupie. Watch arts programmes, profiles and documentaries on writers; listen to **Front Row** on Radio Four as you make your supper and **A Good Read** as you drive to pick up the kids; tune in to **Book Club** on a Sunday afternoon; read A Life in the Day in The *Sunday Times* and listen to **Desert Island Discs**, both of which often feature writers. Read book reviews, even if you can't read all of the books; watch the **South Bank Show** and **Omnibus, Arena** and the **Booker Prize** TV coverage.

I don't think it matters one jot if these writers are people you even read or particularly like, they're *all* grist for the mill. You might just recognise in them facets of what it is that you are trying to find in yourself.

What works for you? What makes you fecund (or not)? Do you need to walk to sort out plot? Do you work best in the morning? Ninety-nine out of every hundred writers I've ever read say that they do, including Garrison Keillor (**Lake Wobegon Days**) and Michael Dobbs, (**House of Cards,** 1991).

Do you need music to work? Alan Sillitoe (**Saturday Night and Sunday Morning**, 1958) listens to Handel's *Messiah*, 'partly for inspiration, partly for white noise.' Esther Freud (The **Gaglow**, 1991) needs silence; Angela Huth, writing **Easy Silence** (2001) listened only to string quartets; Hanif Kureishi (**Intimacy**, 1998) listens to rock music at full volume, while Christopher Brookmyre, (**Country of the Blind**, 1997) 'has to have quiet'.

And just how many drafts is reasonable? Lynda LaPlante (**Cold Heart**, 1999) says she does 'up to sixteen.' Although Tim Lott did the first draft of **White City Blue** (1999) in only two months, it took him three years to complete it, as he reckons he re-wrote it 'a thousand times'.

Should you plan your work in detail, like Michael Dobbs, who says that 'planning and research is where the effort is – writing is less than 50% of my time', and Ken Follett, (**The Key to Rebecca,** 1980) who plots the story chapter by chapter, and then goes over that 'at least a hundred times ...' before he starts writing.

Do you maintain strict order in your study, like Jim Crace, (**Quarantine,** 1998) who thinks his tidiness might be 'an attempt to tame the essential wildness of fiction,' or write in your dressing gown, fingerless mittens, and a blanket around your shoulders, like Wendy Perriam, whose fourteen novels include **Second Skin** (1998).

PD James writes her first draft in long-hand, because she likes the idea of words 'coming down my arm onto the page.' Martin

Amis also does first drafts in pen and ink because, 'You're able to see the history of what you're writing and the corrections bear their own archaeology.'

Tim Lott claims that computers have made writers much better, and thinks that 'even Tolstoy would have benefited from rewriting a few more times.'

If you're writing in a vacuum, you might well think that no one else can be working in the same peculiar way that you do. It's reassuring, then, to find that every writer has foibles, habits, rituals, superstitions and routines.

I've published a few books now, but I still love writers and being around them. You don't have to be in London, they're everywhere. Recently, I went to a talk given by Alan Sillitoe in Wrexham. I've heard Poet Laureate Andrew Motion talk about Philip Larkin, and Jeremy Treglowan discuss Roald Dahl, both in Waterstone's on Muswell Hill.

I've listened to Melvyn Bragg read from his novel, **Credo** (1997) in Hampstead, heard Jeanette Winterson at the National Theatre, crime writer Val McDermid (**The Mermaids Singing,** 1995) at a secondary school in Cheshire and Colin Dexter in a Manchester hotel.

Fortunately, I can run into my friends, TV screenwriter Peter Lloyd, (**Silent Witness; The Bill,**) and radio and stage dramatist Neil Rhodes in my local pub most Friday evenings!

For bizarre locations, though, perhaps attending Ayub Khan's workshop, (writer of the movie, **East is East**) in a Harry Ramsden's chip shop in Manchester takes the batter.

So, if you want to be a writer, meet writers. Go and listen to them and hear what they have to say. Ask them where they like to write, and how; what kind of pencil they use, when they sleep and whether they have to take a walk at noon; drink coffee or vodka, smoke cigarettes, or not.

It makes no difference if they're dull: I've heard writers give readings and talks which would put any normal person off reading – and writing – for life. But you're probably *not* normal, not if you want to be a writer.

Writing's a rollercoaster. There are ups and downs, joys and sorrows. For most of us, it'll be sorrows. Many of the writers that you meet will have their tales of woe and rejection, too. At the very least, it'll be some comfort to know that you're not alone.

Tips and Summary:

1) If you're thinking of being a writer, get out and meet writers.
2) It'll encourage you to stay home and, hopefully, not to write that book

HOW TO … BOOKS

'There's nothing to writing. All you do is sit down at a type-writer and open a vein.'

Red Smith

There are any number of books on the market that claim to be able to tell you how to write a bestseller. I know quite a few writers, including some who have written bestsellers. They're a mixed bunch, male and female, British and American, tall and short, gay and hetero. but they have one thing in common: none of them has learned to do what it is they do by reading a book about it.

One of the main reasons that I am writing this book is that, after my first couple of novels were published, I wondered whether writing a book had to be quite the hard and difficult business that I found it.

Two books down, therefore, I nipped down to the bookstore and bought half a dozen *How to* … guides and ploughed through them.

The *How to* books that I consulted were full of stuff about creating character, writing dialogue, plot points, climaxes and style.

Not only did they not make it any easier for me to write my next book, they would (had I tried to follow their guidance) have positively paralysed me with their advice on how to write.

So depressing, so wholly *inapplicable* to the business of writing as I know it did I find them, that I resolved to write a book, not telling would-be writers *how* to do it, but simply how, for this writer at least, it actually *is*.

One of them – and I am not joking – actually suggested that a writer should consider the appearance of the text on the first page, lest its appearance be off-putting to a potential reader/purchaser.

My advice would be to avoid any of the reassuringly large

number of books that claim to be able to tell you how to write a bestseller, especially if they're by someone you've never heard of.

And avoid at all costs books, invariably American, which have been written by teachers of creative writing in California, and which feature dedications such as: 'To my authors...' or one Roselle Angwin's: 'Offered, as it is, with love and thanks to all those who made it through to the end of the novel course in Plymouth through the winter of 1997/8.'

Books come from within. You really cannot write to a specific plan (beyond the obvious things such as having an outline of the plot and the characters etc.).

Every writer I know goes up blind alleys and round cul-de-sacs in their struggle to get the book out of them. For most of us, the book just has to *evolve*.

This, of course, is not what many would-be writers want to hear, any more than someone learning to drive would want to be told that there are very few rules, and that they'll probably have to have a few (expensive) crashes before they'll learn how to do it.

But writing a novel isn't like driving a car.

Yes, I would recommend that you have some road sense, and that you've seen how cars behave and travel, in the same way that I'd recommend any would-be writer should start by writing shorter pieces before beginning a novel of eighty or ninety thousand words. I'd also recommend that writers manqué do some reading to see how other practitioners do it. As Debra Isaac, a reader for a London literary agency says, 'I wonder why would-be authors never seem to have read published authors ...'

Beyond that, get writing, start crashing into the obstacles that most of us find the road to publication is littered with and, eventually, with practice, you'll work out how to avoid at least some of them, how to make detours and take short-cuts and how to plan your journey so that you don't drive off the road with weariness and exhaustion.

Tips and Summary:

1) Read other writers
2) Avoid *How to...* books
3) Get it written, don't get it right

IDEAS

'I've not had a new idea for the last twenty years.'

CEM Joad

'Where do you get your ideas from?' is one of the questions that writers are asked repeatedly, and is one of the most difficult to answer. It's very difficult to say *where* they come from, and if one knew, one would return again and again to that well, and simply haul up the bucket with a good idea splashing about in it.

Although I'm not sure *where* they come from, I do know what quite a number of writers have said about how they foster ideas, how they try to free up the creative mind, and make it receptive to any ideas that might be in the air.

Joseph Heller (**Catch 22,** 1961; **Something Happened,** 1974) maintained that he had 'to be alone. A bus is good. Or walking the dog. Brushing my teeth is marvellous…'

Many writers find that walking is essential to their creative process. Dickens pounded the streets of London for hours at a time.

Newscaster turned thriller writer, Gerald Seymour, walks with his dogs every day, and even tries out chunks of dialogue on them.

In a programme broadcast on Radio Four in 2002, *Three Miles an Hour*, presenter William Dalrymple spoke to many writers – including novelist Helen Dunmore, poet John Burnside, Bruce Chatwin's widow, Elizabeth, and crime novelist Reginald Hill – all of whom said that walking was essential for their work. They may not necessarily come up with ideas, (although Hill did, on one occasion, come up with a story that was subsequently made into an American TV movie) but the consensus was that the very motion of putting one foot in front of the other freed up the mind, and all sorts of issues and plot problems, as well as actual ideas, tended to fall into place.

Hill often takes a dictaphone with him, fearing that he might forget the idea he has had, whereas Burnside reckons that the strength of a poem he might begin to compose can be tested by whether he can still remember it by the time he is back home.

Naturalist and thinker, Henry David Thoreau (**Walden,** 1854) tramped the woods around Walden Pond in Connecticut for four or five hours every day, and thought he would be ill if he were not allowed to do so.

It may be true that there are only seven basic plots in the world, but many writers find that this is one of the very best things that they can do to tease out a new spin on one of them.

I know from my own experience that when I've got a crime novel underway, I frequently run into blind alleys and what can seem intractable plot problems. It is then that I find it invaluable to walk. There seems to be something about the solitary motion, the mindless trudge (in city or country) in which the very planting of one foot in front of the other combines with the processes of the mind to free up the creative juices, the juices which, according to Dorothea Brande (**Becoming a Writer,** Macmillan) are ready and willing to flow, if we will only allow them to do so.

The other essential activity to facilitate the fostering of ideas (and the resolution of difficulties) is, of course, sleep. I've often gone to bed exhausted with trying to work out some plot problem, only to find that on waking the next morning, the answer has arrived, unbidden. The fact that the answer seems both ingenious and simple is even more remarkable.

This is just one of the reasons why prudent writers keep a pad beside their bed. There's no need to be the Alan Alda character in Woody Allen's *Crimes and Misdemeanours,* where every half-baked thought and idea that the man has is spoken into his ever-present voice recorder; just a discreet little notebook near at hand will do.

I've also been struck, listening to writers, or reading accounts of their childhoods, by how many of them spent a lot of time alone, frequently isolated by either sickness or family circumstances.

Not surprisingly, perhaps, this kind of enforced solitude (often an unhappy period) seems to facilitate the growth of the imagination and provide a rich source of ideas.

*

Whilst walking's a great idea, and one recommended by any number of writers – including Ian McEwan – where your writing is concerned, it really is best to keep quiet whilst you're doing it. Angus Wilson (**Anglo Saxon Attitudes,** 1956) said, 'If I communicate the magic spell…it loses its force for me.'

Every writer I have ever known, and all those that I have read about, keep the first draft of their projects (apart from the barest outline, perhaps) firmly under their hats. Talk it through, and it will be flat and tired on the page. It's a horrible sensation to have felt so enthusiastic about a project, and then to find that as the words appear on the screen, they are listless and stale.

Ideas are gold dust, and they're not for scattering in the wind of talk. Walk all you like, but don't talk, no matter how strong the temptation.

As well as walking (alone, of course) I find that solitary journeys are good for my juices. It can be trains (the best), buses, boats or cars, but not planes: I'm such an anxious flier that I need all my concentration to keep the thing in the air, and there's no relaxed space left to let ideas take shape.

Any kind of motion, or any kind of repetitive, desultory activity is good: painting; sawing wood (excellent); hoeing the vegetable patch or weeding between the beans (wonderful). But it has to be something undemanding, solitary and silent. Something that

131

engages the body at a very rudimentary level, but which leaves the mind free; something that involves humdrum routine, silence and motion. Try a few of these things, and you'll eventually find what it is that works for you. And then nurture it. Don't neglect it, but do it.

*

The germ of the idea behind each of my books has been different. The idea for **Night's Black Agents** crept up on me. The tale of my grandmother's liaison with one of the customers in the pub that she and my grandfather ran in Birmingham in the 1920s was an open family secret.

During the years, as I cast around (unconsciously) for a story that might support the length of a novel, this one must have seeped into my consciousness and attracted to it, like filings to a magnet, other imagined elements.

The setting appealed. The city, in the early part of the century, was far enough away for me to enjoy imagining and researching facets of life there. The couple of images that I had from my mother were both powerful and poignant. She, as a young child at an upstairs window, the noise and colour and hubbub of the public house below. Her witnessing the dislocated relationship of her parents, and the beauty of her adulterous mother, drawn by the power of lust to another man, her mild-mannered husband, tortured by the brazen affair.

It was also long enough ago (the main characters in the story were deceased) for me to write about it without fear of hurting others, and with the possibility of embellishing the story to make it more dramatic, and to develop the consequences of the actual affair into a murderous fictional tale.

Funnily enough, had **Night's Black Agents** been accepted sooner, rather than later, I'd probably have been engaged on writing a whole series featuring a 1930's Birmingham Detective Inspector rather than several stand-alone novels.

My second book, **Less Than Kind,** drew on a formative period in my own life. In 1968, my then-girlfriend and myself put all our belongings in the back of a hired van and drove from Cromwell Road in London's Earls Court, where we were living just down the road from the BA terminal, and headed for a cottage in mid-Wales.

I'd been driving a lorry delivering building supplies, and Penny had been working as a secretary at St Mary's Hospital in Paddington. A colleague in her office had told her that if we wanted to go and live in the countryside, there were any number of cottages available in the area of Montgomeryshire where she came from.

She was right. The night we arrived, we were shown three abandoned cottages, any one of which we could take on for a peppercorn rent. It was March. There was a dusting of snow on the ground, sheep with their lambs in the garden, and stout daffodils in the hedgerow. It was magical.

Those times, some of the happiest of my life, are deeply etched in my mind, and when I came to write my second book – even as the first was being rejected by publishers – it was to that time and place that I returned.

The story I wrote was about this sylvan idyll being sullied by incoming gangsters from the city. In fact, as the book makes clear, the things that were going on in the remote and silent countryside were every bit as tawdry as anything that came by black Mercedes down those country lanes.

Because I knew the area intimately, even though the book was written many years after the time that I had lived there, I was pleased with a deal of it, particularly the bits that relate to the countryside.

The city-set bits are less successful; they're thin and shaky and lack conviction, because I hadn't been fully assimilated into the

London milieu. No matter, it's a fairly complex plot, and some of it is rendered reasonably powerfully.

Until Dawn Tomorrow was about a serial-killing wronged lover, and sprung pretty directly from my own experiences of going through divorce. They say fiction is 95% autobiography.

Thought For The Day is a sort of recovery novel. I was in a new relationship, in a new city (London) and with my senses open to a lot of new experiences. It's a tale of fraud, kidnap and murder set around the brittle, shiny world of advertising.

On this occasion, I did have the germ of the idea from an independent source. In 1989, I'd read the story of a man who had tried to perpetrate a big insurance fraud. He was going to drive his Mercedes into Lake Como and disappear. But instead of escaping from the car, he drowned in it.

I wanted to use the man's story for the ending of **Thought For The Day**. What I had to do was work out a story that would lead me to this climax, a sort of working from the end back to the beginning.

The idea behind **Small Vices** was very loosely inspired by my seeing a TV documentary about a gang of men who spend the year roaming the country painting electric pylons. This was an interesting and, as far as I was aware, original idea. (In fact, although I didn't know it at the time, Simon Beaufoy, writer of *The Full Monty*, wrote *Among Giants* (1998) a movie starring Pete Postlethwaite and set in the same milieu at about the same time as I was writing my book.)

These men travel, they work in some danger, and under tough physical conditions. The imagination started to run. The possibilities within this little-known 'community', the sort of men who might be attracted to it, the opportunities for blokeish behaviour, living in a dirty and difficult environment (caravans etc.), and being away from their wives and girlfriends for longish periods seemed to me pregnant with possibilities.

The pylon painters, as it happens, don't play a huge role in the story, but they are there as a backdrop, and their itinerant lifestyle allows the murderer (one of their number) to be difficult for the police to identify and catch.

One of the worries frequently articulated by would-be authors is that script editors, publishers' readers (often writers themselves), directors, and just about anyone else who gets to read their work, might steal it.

The problem is that ideas cannot be protected and copyrighted, and so once your book/film idea is shown to people, it can, conceivably, be borrowed from, adapted, or plain stolen. It's a worrying thought.

But, realistically, what choice does a writer have? We all assume we've written a masterpiece (God knows, we wouldn't have slogged at it for a year or more if we didn't) and we're naturally pretty sure that any publisher getting a sight of it will want to rush it into print on our behalf.

The reality is, sadly, rather different. You have almost certainly *not* written the new **Harry Potter**, and it's very likely that your desire to be published will require you to implore people to read your manuscript, and accept *their* terms for doing so, rather than dictating your own.

But, early days, flushed with enthusiasm and self-belief, it's likely that, like the rest of us, you'll be very choosy about who you show your novel to. And, whether you're the new JK Rowling or not, to you, this manuscript is a very important thing, and it'd be strange if you didn't treasure it as such.

As for your novel being stolen, this is highly unlikely. Apart from anything else, unless you show it to a publisher who's going to steal your manuscript (written in English) and then have it translated into Urdu and distribute it exclusively to the Pushtan tribes of inaccessible areas of Afghanistan, his scam will soon be exposed. And if it isn't exposed, it means that your book has not

135

been a roaring success. No, your book won't be nicked. It just doesn't happen.

The germ, the *idea* behind a book or story or film, though, is a more difficult thing. And yes, here, there is some risk of plagiarism. If someone actually appropriates your plot and dialogue and characters, you can sue them for plagiarism, but if they appropriate your idea, there's little that you can do.

In any event, at all costs, avoid legal action. Court cases are long, time-consuming and very, very expensive.

Better to take the advice that Charles Dickens offers about court proceedings in **Bleak House**: 'Suffer any wrong that can be done to you, rather than come here!'

No, don't go to court if you can possibly avoid it. And certainly don't unless you are absolutely rock solid about your facts and information.

One of the reasons that ideas sometimes *appear* to have been stolen, adapted or re-written is the *zeitgeist*.

Ideas knock around and come around at the same time because similar people, often of similar ages and backgrounds, in the media, journalism and the arts, are often thinking about similar things at the same time.

There are often sound, practical/historical reasons for this. The time-delayed releasing of government papers relating to a particular topic might well lead to several writers setting to work on plays or books based on a specific issue from history, all at the same time.

Just recently, after years of relative artistic silence on the topic, there have been two major TV dramas by leading TV playwrights on the subject of northern Ireland's so-called Bloody Sunday. A similar thing happened with the Hillsborough football stadium tragedy.

In 1991, after what had been little film interest in things coming out of Sherwood forest, two big-production Robin Hood movies,

Robin: Prince of Thieves and *Robin Hood*, were released within weeks of one another.

A similar thing happened with *1492*, and *Columbus* in the early 1990's. There had been little Hollywood interest in the exploits of C. Columbus until then, but when some film executive thought that the 500th anniversary of the Spaniard's exploits might be a good time to put him on screen, we had two big movies produced at the same time.

And sometimes there is pure *coincidence*.

But more often – and this is the difficult-to-prove area – writers will sometimes subconsciously absorb material from other sources. I certainly do it myself, and it's one of the reasons that many writers do not read fiction when they are writing it. It's incredibly easy to soak up another writer's style, (if not their actual content,) and find that you have lost, overnight, the distinctive voice of your own work. For this reason I would recommend you read only biography and letters, diaries and memoirs when you're writing your novel.

It's all too easy, having taken in a story from the TV news, a newspaper article or, worst of all, another piece of fiction that we have read somewhere, (often long ago) to subconsciously squirrel it away, and later write something believing it to be original when, in fact, it has been 'borrowed' without our knowing it.

A few years ago, it was remarked how similar PD James's 1994 **Original Sin** (at that time, number one in the bestseller list) was to **End of Chapter,** a book written forty years previously by the then-Poet Laureate, C. Day-Lewis under the pseudonym Nicholas Blake.

Was it mere coincidence, critics wondered, that both books were set in publishers' offices on the River Thames? Each book begins with someone turning up early for an appointment at the publishers, and the murder victims in both books include a former best-selling authoress who is now past her best.

PD James claimed that these, and other similarities between the two books, were mere coincidence: 'Ideas float around and get caught by different people,' she said, adding that, whatever defects she might have as a writer, lack of ideas was not one of them: 'There are only a limited number of plots, and thousands of writers.'

A few years after this, science fiction writer Brian Aldiss raised questions about similarities between the same writer (PD James's) 2000 novel, **The Children of Men**, and his own book, **Greybeard**, published in 1964. He later said that the similarities had been a 'curious coincidence,' and that since then, he had found that he had *himself* unconsciously plagiarised a friend's story.

At about the same time, David Lodge (**Therapy**, 1995; **Changing Places**, 1975; **Thinks**, 2002) accused a Mills and Boon writer of plagiarising his 1989 novel, **Nice Work**, in her book, **The Iron Master**.

The author was dropped by her publisher and sued Lodge; he subsequently retracted his accusation and apologised.

But all said and done, I do believe, much more often than not, that mistakes of this sort are exactly that: mistakes.

One can understand very well the irritation that any author might feel if he thinks that his material is being usurped. After all, whilst many writers can turn a phrase, ideas are pretty elusive, and good ideas are incredibly difficult to find.

I know from my own experience just how difficult it is not to absorb and recycle material. I have sometimes started to jot down ideas, or written outlines and even half-chapters, thinking I was writing original material, only to subsequently find that I was re-hashing something that I'd jotted down a dozen years previously, often using the very same phrases and sentences in both drafts.

The thing that is most likely to ensure the safety of your novel or script, though, is this simple fact: why on earth, if you've submitted a good book or play or film script, should the publisher or TV/film company *want* to steal it? Remember the old joke about the Hollywood starlet who was so stupid she slept with the writer? Fact is, writers aren't usually short-changed of their material, because they're at the bottom of the food chain anyway: they don't get paid enough to make it worth anyone's while *not* to pay them.

And because good ideas *aren't* that thick on the ground, people will (assuming that they have the wit to recognise your work as half decent) be delighted to pay you for it, rather than sneak it off to someone else and get them to re-write it.

And yes, of course, if people in publishing and the media are reading dozens of manuscripts a week, there will be occasions where similar ideas will arise, and similar stories get written. And yes, some of these hundreds of ideas/manuscripts/outlines and proposals will slip through into conferences and meetings and will, eventually, go through the mixer and come out as something not entirely dissimilar. But it's very rarely by design. I met someone recently who, at the height of the fame of the cartoon, *Bob the Builder*, claimed to have submitted an identical idea to the BBC years before the eponymous hero made his appearance. And I'm sure she was speaking the truth. What *actually* happened, no one, of course, will ever know.

Tips and Summary:

1) There are only a limited number of ideas in the world.
2) The writer's task is to find a new spin to put on one of them.
3) Similar ideas do tend to pop up at the same time.
4) It's unlikely your idea will be stolen by a publisher/TV company: it's cheaper to pay you to write it.
5) Even if you think someone's nicked your plot, stay away from the Old Bailey.

THE JOY OF IT ALL

'KILL YOUR DARLINGS' ... (AND OTHER CLICHÉS)

I've paid lip-service to this bon-mot of William Faulkner's for years. After all, it's one of those clichés about writing that is endlessly trotted out.

Samuel Johnson's, *'Read over your compositions, and wherever you meet with a passage which you think is particularly fine, strike it out,'* is the 18th century version of the same idea.

In **On the Art of Writing**, in 1914, Sir Arthur Quiller-Couch said, *'Whenever you feel an impulse to perpetrate a piece of exceptionally fine writing, obey it – wholeheartedly – and delete it before sending your manuscript to press. Murder your darlings.'*

And even today, novelist James Hawes (**A White Merc With Fins,** 1996; **Rancid Aluminium,** 1998) is still repeating it: *'I always tell friends who are writers that it's crucial to get rid of stuff that you like because it's probably weak and only in there because you like it.'*

Sorry? *Only in there because you like it?* Just what is this proscribing of the words, sentences and phrases that you *like?* Can this really be sensible advice?

It was Johnson who also gave us the even more frequently recycled: *'No man but a blockhead ever wrote, except for money.'* This has always struck me as not only syntactically awkward, but patently untrue.

Yes, of course writing is hard, and frequently unrewarding, but as we all know, many of the greatest works of art have been undertaken because the artist felt he or she simply *had* to do the work.

That artist may well have died poor, unhappy, and (frequently) mad, but they could no more have taken Johnson's advice than their counterparts can take it today.

Writers write. Whether it's Jeffrey Archer, locked up in Lincoln prison, Alexander Solzhenitsyn writing **One Day in the Life of Ivan Denisovich** (1971), or Czech author Ivan Klima (**Lovers for the Day,** 1999) who said, 'I'd still write if I couldn't get published. Even when my work was banned I still wrote.'

Although it's probably unique to see Archer and Solzhenitsyn's names used in the same paragraph, in fairness to the disgraced peer, many critics thought that **The Prison Diary of Jeffrey Archer** (2002) was his best book. Its publication meant a loss of both remission and privileges for Archer, and the incentive, apparently, was not financial (the proceeds being donated to charity) but rather his *need* to write.

'*Kill your darlings*,'? Any half-decent writer knows when he or she has done good work. When I'm reading my stuff in draft, or when I'm giving a reading, I know when there's a tasty paragraph hoving into view. I know it, and I'm glad. Because I trust my judgement about my own work, just as I trust my judgement about other writers' prose. And no, of course I'm not going to delete it just because I'm pleased with it.

Of course, if you are writing a book which you hope readers will want to read for the texture of the prose, and the nuances of characters' behaviour, but your editor is expecting a fast-moving, racy thriller, a book whose pace is not to be arrested by your perceptive observations and subtle insights, there will clearly be problems ahead.

If she wants one-dimensional characters who are moving at pace through a changing landscape, and you are trying to write elegant prose in a leisurely style, then maybe you are writing the wrong book for the wrong publisher.

I'm not suggesting that measured prose is going to make for a good book, any more than I believe that a fast-paced book that is plot-driven is necessarily a bad one. It's simply a good idea to know *which* it is that you are trying to write.

The problem with the kind of thinly-characterised crime novel which I personally find difficult to read is that, although they are often termed *Whodunnits,* for this reader, they are *Who gives a damn who done its?* For, unless I'm involved with the characters, how can I possibly care about what happens to them?

Friends often tell me, when I say I've found this or that best-selling novel virtually unreadable (Alex Garland's **The Beach,** 1997; Tony Parsons's **Man and Boy,** 2000) that, 'You have to admit, though, it's a great story.'

Well, of course, it *may* be a good story, but unfortunately, I'll never know because I've not cleared the first hurdle of being convinced of the 'truth' of the characters or the veracity of the prose and so haven't been able to read it.

PD James puts it succinctly when she says: 'It doesn't matter how exciting a book is: if it's badly written one just can't be bothered with it.'

There's one rule of 'criticism' that I fall back on again and again: 'I don't know what it was *like*, but I know it wasn't like *this*.' Whether I'm watching the TV adaptation of George Eliot's 1876 **Daniel Deronda**, or in the theatre watching **King Lear**, it's the only star I use to guide me: Was it like this?

I wasn't in England in the twelfth century, (or whenever it is that **King Lear**'s supposedly set) but the essential truth of what Cordelia and Gloucester and the irascible old King do and say and feel doesn't ever make me question the truth of that play.

I don't care how good a story it is claimed that Alex Garland is telling in **The Beach,** I simply couldn't read it. No one in the history of the world has ever said/done such things in quite those ways, no matter how far from home and how many drugs they've taken. This was not *true*.

With my book sales in thousands and Garland's in millions, he must be right. But I still don't believe it. Arrogant or what?

Writing is re-writing. That *is* true.

But, no, don't *murder your darlings*. Subject them, just as you would your own children, to fair-minded scrutiny. If they're found wanting, chide them; banish them, even, but don't let them go simply because you love them.

In early drafts, I always over-write. It's how it happens for me. I value that gush of words not because they're right, but because without them on the page, I've nothing at all.

Experience has taught me this. It's also taught me that three, four or five drafts later, I will have cut a lot of this material, but there will still be a lot more to cut.

I know this, because when I do it, the work reads more crisply, and it reads right.

There's a difference between this and taking out the things that you like simply *because* you like them. A big difference.

Blockheads? Money? Well, that *might* be a different story. Why not play safe? Don't write at all, whether for money or anything else.

Tips and Summary:

1) For every bit of advice, every proverb, bon-mot and epigram, there's another that baldly contradicts it. It's up to you which you choose.

LAUNCHES

'The good thing about writing fiction is that you can get back at people.'

John Grisham

The book launches that we get to see or read about are the glamorous affairs where the glitterati show up at a smart London venue, sip champagne and pick at canapés before, half an hour later, they are driven off into the night in black Mercedes.

That's fine, of course, if you're Victoria Beckham or Jamie Oliver. There are even a very few *writers* (i.e., people who are writers, first and foremost, as opposed to footballers, chefs or pop stars,) who are media attractions themselves: JK Rowling and Bill Bryson, for example, authors who can, simply on the strength of their books' success, pull in huge crowds.

Writers like Nick Hornby, Alan Bennett, Irvine Welsh, Jilly Cooper and Howard Marks are popular enough to fill a hall or a theatre for a reading, and even charge readers a fiver for the privilege of being there.

And then, a very long way behind, there's the rest of us.

And when it comes to *our* book launches, we are in a dilemma.

Unless you're one of the aforementioned celebrities, or a writer with a really considerable following, and sales to match, the very words 'book launch' will send a chill down the spine of your publishers.

My editor told me he'd recently been to the launch of a literary title at a prestigious London venue. At the end of the evening, he bought a copy of the author's new book. 'How has it been?' he asked. 'It's been great,' said the chuffed writer, 'We've sold twenty-*five* copies.'

For most of us 'midlisters', writers with a few books to our name, this does constitute a successful launch.

But, as someone who is resident outside London – as many writers are – I'd suggest that this is one of those rare occasions when we can turn our out-of-town status to our advantage. When it comes to book launches, small *can* be beautiful, a market town a much better bet than a West End venue.

In 1993, when my first book was published, I felt so cock-a-hoop that I wanted to celebrate and thank all those friends and family who had been supportive in my own particular getting published saga.

HarperCollins were sceptical. 'A book launch? In *Shropshire?*'

I persuaded them to do the invitations. I cajoled a reluctant local bookseller to order a few boxes of **Night's Black Agents** (sale or return) and to turn up on the evening at the town's biggest hotel.

I ordered the wine. The invitations were for seven-thirty. I didn't put RSVP on them, thinking that people were more likely to stick it on the mantlepiece and then, on the evening (try to choose a weekday evening, of course, and not one on which United are playing a big European Cup game) they might think, 'Well, there's not much on telly, shall we …?'

As the day approached, a few people seemed to be crossing the road to avoid me, but most of those I bumped into said they were looking forward to coming. One friend phoned and said, 'I've never been to a book launch before, what do I wear?' I had to tell him I'd never been to one either!

At seven-thirty, the hotel function room had two people in it: the bookseller and myself. He'd got a little display in the far corner of the room (nothing too overt) and we made small talk as I tried to disguise my discomfiture at what was obviously going to be an embarrassing evening.

He wandered away to fiddle with the books on the table. At seven-forty, as if someone had opened a gate outside, people flocked in. It was amazing. They absolutely poured through the doors. Yes, I know the few writers who live locally, and they were there, but there were also my five-a-side football mates; ex-teacher colleagues; solicitors; estate agents, truck drivers and doctors.

The hubbub of noise grew, the atmosphere filled and coloured and softened, there were smiles and greetings everywhere. It felt as if everyone, not just myself, was congratulating themselves on the apparent success of the event.

My dad and my mother-in-law; Bernard and Sue who run the florist's; Carole and ambulance-man-husband, Harry. Even Ron and Pauline who run the local pub. Here was the world and his wife.

The bookseller sold over *fifty* hardback copies of **Night's Black Agents** and, at the end of the evening, took me aside and handed me fifty quid towards the wine. I know this is very minor league compared with the big players, but to sell that number of hardback copies of your book not only feels very affirming, it also sends it off with a bit of a bang and gives the local media something to hang their local author/new book story on.

After that first book, the local launch parties have become something of a tradition. People sometimes stop me on the street and ask me how the new book is coming along, not so much out of any 'literary' interest, I'm sure, but because they are looking forward to the next party.

Of course, five novels and nine years on, the invitation list's become a logistical nightmare: one or two people have actually died, many have divorced, people have left town, emigrated, run away from this or that; new folk have arrived.

And this last time, just two days before the 'do' for the new novel, **Small Vices**, there *were* no books. Printed in Spain, there was a delay as they were being flown to Stansted. For a while, it looked as if this might be that unique event, a book launch with no books. They did arrive eventually, with hours to spare.

At the party, there was the usual eclectic mix of folk: liggers and freeloaders, local writers and family, footy players, dentists, builders, taxmen and teachers. It felt good and, even though it's a party to celebrate the book's publication, and not an event merely to sell books, every copy that the publisher dispatched (all sixty of them) sold out, with orders taken for a couple of dozen more.

So, book launches and signings: if you're a celebrity, your publisher will hire a PR firm, order the champagne and smoked salmon, and book a ritzy, West End joint.

No one, of course, will be leaving with a copy of your book in a paper bag. But that's not what the event's for.

But if, like most writers, you're 'midlist', and you live outside of London, I'd suggest you stay close to home: it'll be a nice atmosphere and, (if you're lucky,) you might just sell some books!

Tips and Summary:

1) Don't write the book: you won't have to have a party
2) If you insist on writing it, and it gets published (unlikely), splash out and have a party.
3) There's bound be a few enemies in the crowd who will be seething with jealousy at your triumph. Think of it as money well spent.
4) You might even sell a few books

LUCK

'…if we could see all, all might seem good.'
Edward Thomas

Everything else is negotiable: a bit of talent; a bit of discipline; a bit of an idea. But you've *got* to have some luck. Without it, unless you're so extraordinarily talented, so well-placed, so connected that you just can't fail, nothing happens.

George Ewart Evans, who wrote ten books for Faber & Faber about the Suffolk countryside and its inhabitants, had some. Just.

Evans had been enduring the miseries of supply teaching and struggling, with his wife, also a teacher, to write and bring up four children – one of whom, Matthew, went on to become chairman of Faber – in a Suffolk village.

Recording the reminiscences of these village people, he sent the manuscript of **Ask the Fellows Who Cut the Hay** (1965) to Faber where it was read by Jan Perkins, a publisher's reader.

She added a note to the bottom of Ewart Evans' accompanying letter, 'If he were not so revoltingly pompous and pedantic, this book might be interesting for the way of life it recaptures. As it stands it is dulled by the author's personal interpolations.'

Ewart Evans' letter, duly annotated by Ms Perkins, was sent to an editor, Morley Kennerley, an American director of Faber's, along with the manuscript.

Kennerley subsequently added to the letter, 'this book is a joy … most readable, nothing patronising about it,' and added that, with regard to its being revoltingly pompous '…nothing could be further from the truth'.

The book, and many more by George Ewart Evans, was published by Faber. Thank goodness for the Morley Kennerleys of this world.

In late 1989, I found in my pigeonhole at the college where I was teaching A-level English, an ad clipped from the *Guardian's* careers' page inviting applications to go and work in Saudi Arabia. I was bemused. I had a young family, was (relatively) happy teaching, and spent most evenings working on my novel and other pieces of writing.

At coffee time, I showed the ad to my friend and colleague, Maureen. She gave me an old-fashioned look and turned the piece of paper over in my hand. On the other side was an invitation from comedian Lenny Henry's TV production company to submit scripts to apply for a place on a comedy writers' course that the BBC was jointly organising.

I sent some sketches off. Lots of writers try different areas of writing before finding the one that suits them best.

At this time, I was not only working on my first novel, but was also sending comedy to shows like *Spitting Image,* and performers like Jasper Carrott. I'd recommend this approach to any writer. Try lots of things, have a go at lots of different forms. You never know. It's a lottery, and the most surprising projects sometimes yield unexpected results.

I've done newspaper features (*The Times; Daily Telegraph; Evening Standard; Manchester Evening News*) and had magazine fiction and features published. And, during the last eighteen months, I've had two plays produced.

You will almost certainly have stuff rejected. But if you've only got one project going out and coming back, you will soon despair. If you've got *several* projects on the go, not only have you got more likelihood of success (if any of them are any good!) but it'll keep your mind off the painful business of waiting for a response to your solitary venture.

As well as keeping you sane, your work will improve with the practise and discipline of doing more work. Writing is re-writing. And, who knows, you might find you're not a novelist at all, but a screenplay writer, radio dramatist or, worst of all, a poet: (novelists don't earn much, but most poets earn nothing at all!)

Anyway, I was accepted on Lenny Henry's BBC comedy-writing weekend – one of thirty writers from around the country who had made the cut for the three-day workshop – and made my way down to a hotel in Basingstoke one Friday afternoon.

Henry was there for his TV company, Crucial Films, and Kim Fuller, (brother to Simon Fuller, svengali to the Spice Girls) was there as script editor for us would-be Woody Allens.

When I read the list of speakers, I thought the whole thing must be some kind of con: Richard Curtis, writer of *Blackadder*, and (since then) *Mr Bean, Four Weddings and a Funeral* and *Notting Hill*; comedy executives James Moir and Jonathan Powell; producers Robin Nash (*Bread* and *Reginald Perrin*) and John Lloyd (*Not The Nine O'Clock News, Blackadder* and *Spitting Image*).

But no, it was all kosher. Travel and hotel expenses were being paid. Lenny Henry himself, the force behind the idea – one of whose aims was to attract more black writers into TV – was present for the whole three days, and Dawn French came down for lunch.

Lucky? I could have easily put that ad from the *Guardian* in the bin, and never even seen the piece.

In truth, I found it difficult working under pressure, and trying to come up with stuff on the hoof. It's not really the way I work.

But I did learn a deal of things (one of them being that I'm not really a TV sketch writer) and some of the writers on that course have gone on to be successful comedy writers.

The Basingstoke event led to another, a couple of years later, when Carlton TV invited me down to the plush surroundings of the Anugraha Hotel in Egham for another, similar sort of workshop.

I wrote some stuff during the couple of days we were there, but when I went down to the studios in west London a few months later for the recording of the TV pilot that was to feature our efforts, none of mine was in it, but writers like David Quantick and Jane Bussmann, whom I've frequently heard and seen on TV and radio shows since, were.

No matter. I wasn't overly concerned not to have cut the mustard as a comedy writer. By this time, **Night's Black Agents** was at the printers: I was about to be a novelist!

Summary and Tips:

1) Most luck, you don't even know you've had. Any more than you are aware how close you've been to opportunities you've missed.
2) The harder you practise, the luckier you get? There may be some truth in that, too.
3) Yes, you'll need to practice, but you'll need a bit of luck, too.

MURDER

'What the detective story is about is not murder but the restoration of order.'

PD James

Every genre has its own 'rules'. Science-fiction, romance, Westerns. And if you're going to write in excess of eighty thousand words (about the shortest feasible length for a crime novel) you need a plot, and a crime – or crimes – to sustain it.

The question is, why does it (invariably) have to be the crime of murder or, (increasingly) murders? There are other commandments: about stealing and lying and neighbours' wives, after all.

I don't underestimate the effects of lesser crime on ordinary people, whether it's a pub brawl, a burglary or handbag theft. But it is the taking of another's life that is the ultimate, the capital crime.

It doesn't mean to say that one can't, and that people don't, write about armed robberies and auction heists, counterfeiting and all sorts of drugs scams. But critically, for the crime writer, it is murder that involves the resources and expertise of the most senior detectives in the police force (of whom the crime writer's hero/heroine/main character is likely to be one).

Of course, many of the crimes mentioned above, whilst serious in themselves, also often lead to murder. What starts as rape, blackmail, an abduction or a big drugs deal, frequently leads to killing as the situation escalates in gravity, recklessness, or fear of detection.

And that's why the majority of crime novels deal with murder. The stakes are the highest, the consequences, the greatest.

Of course, real life isn't anything like a few hours with a decent crime novel. As I write, the entire nation is discussing the abduction of two young girls from Cambridgeshire. Their parents are suffering the daily agony of their being 'discovered', as opposed to 'found'. Any parent's heart goes out to them. The police don't *appear* to have been very efficient in conducting the enquiry, with apparent delays in following up the reporting of important leads.

Early sightings and witness 'certainties', though, have subsequently been discounted as erroneous, or wilfully misleading.

This is real life. Searching hedgerows, checking statements, dealing with thousands of calls, staging reconstructions, and going through the mountain of information that clogs the system as people try to 'help'.

In a novel, the enterprising, devious criminal is tracked down by the wily detective and his slow sidekick. In reality, no senior detective gets a hunch and follows it through. The entire team sifts paper, checks statements, clears scrubland and interviews known sex-offenders.

My own contention is that for a novel, the crime has to be serious, usually premeditated, and preferably slightly ingenious. In reality, in the most frequent types of murder – where the victim and perpetrator are known to one another – the cops are too smart, and their forensics and surveillance too sophisticated to allow the killer much chance of evading capture and prosecution.

But novels deal not in criminal statistics, but in fiction, and as long as the crime and motive are plausible, readers will not complain.

I've sat in crown court and watched the ordinariness of the guilty. The bus driver who sexually abused a child, murdered him, and then took it upon himself to befriend the bereaved family and act as their spokesperson to the media.

I've seen the misery of the woman, a member of a suburban local amateur dramatic society who, having had an affair with her leading man, when he threatened to call the relationship off, went to the man's house and bludgeoned his wife to death.

As I write, these people are still in prison, serving their time, their families destroyed for ever. That's the reality. In books, (well, in many of them) corpses stack up like there's no tomorrow, the fall-out from terrible deeds dealt with in a few paragraphs or a couple of pages. In reality, it's not like that; it's not like that at all.

And so, although there are exceptions, generally speaking, crime novelists stick to major crime (murder), with major consequences (life imprisonment) and the most senior officers investigating the cases.

Yes, there is rape and paedophilia, there are serial killers and there is gang warfare, but many writers seem to prefer a contemporary, bloody version of what might be called the Jane Austen template: two or three families and a confined setting. For *that's* what most crimes are about. Motivated by jealousy, passion or money, people either commit a murder themselves, or hire someone (often highly unreliable) to do it for them.

But their secrets – the illicit affair, their partner's infidelity, the increased life insurance cover, are quickly rumbled. And then, how do they explain the withdrawals from the building society? The long distance telephone calls? The unaccounted-for absences? The credit card payment for this or that gift?

The suspect has little chance once they are on this slippery slope. The cops wear them down. They say that to be a good liar you have to have a very good memory. You can go over the true version of events a hundred times and you won't be found out, for there's nothing *to* be found out. You might add a line, drop a phrase, but if it's true, if it's what happened, you can't be faulted.

But if you are telling a lie, you only have to muddle a tense or misplace a word, and those attentive cops will sniff out your error in a moment.

Yes, even today, murder's still the crime.

Tips and Summary:

1) Don't do it (write that book)
2) Don't do it (murder)

NAMES

'No, Groucho is not my real name. I'm breaking it in for a friend.'

Groucho Marx

Martin Amis reckons that if you're going to spend two or three hundred pages with a character, write his name hundreds – possibly thousands – of times, it's a good idea to get something that really fits.

Dickens, according to his biographer, Peter Ackroyd, could not write a character until he had a fitting name. And what a legacy of grotesques he left us: Micawber; Fagin; Estelle Haversham; Tulkinghorn; Magwitch, and a hundred other extraordinary names and characters that have become part of the English language itself.

But beware, unless you are planning on writing a classic – a book in which you can probably get away with someone like Trollope's creation in **Barchester Towers**, the wonderfully-named 'Obadiah Slope' – names are as susceptible to fashion as anything else.

I grimace at the wedding photos of myself in my wide-lapelled suit, brown shirt and terrible 'kipper' tie, and wish I had simply gone to Moss Bros. and hired a morning suit like generations before me. You might, therefore, do well to choose a 'Moss Brothers' name for your central character unless you, too, want your *zeitgeist* novel to look beached by the tides of fashion in only a few years time.

The best approach is to give your main character a name that feels comfortable to you, that you're at ease with, and that you aren't going to mind typing a thousand times. It should, also, be a name that goes some way to reflecting that person's character: Sue Townsend's eponymous 'Adrian Mole'; the central character in

159

Martin Amis's **Money** (1984) 'John Self', with all that that sobriquet implies; the 'hero' of his **London Fields** (1989), dart-playing, drink-sodden, 'Keith Talent'.

Many of Evelyn Waugh's novels feature a character called Crutweed. This unfortunate was a former university tutor of the novelist's. Waugh disliked the man so much that the don has now achieved a sort of dubious immortality in the satirist's novels.

Simon Gray's **Old Flames** actually names the theatre critics who had so irritated the playwright that he finally takes the opportunity to level the score. (Quite a risky strategy, I'd have thought, and not one I'd recommend to a budding writer.)

When I look at the books I've had published, I regret that I didn't take *more* care over names. In **Night's Black Agents**, set in the 1930s, I called my Birmingham-based detective, 'John Hammond'. This was unexceptionable. But really, I know that I could have done better. (The villain, a taciturn boatman, 'Ezra Talbot', was both more fittingly and more engagingly named.)

In my second book, the 1960s-set **Less Than Kind,** the hero-cop is 'John Munroe'. A little better, I think, but really, it says nothing about the man, it's so unadventurous, so anonymous.

At least with the first book, I have the excuse that the book was written as much in hope as expectation: I was by no means sanguine about its success in finding a publisher.

But by the time **Less Than Kind** was written, I had a publisher, and that book was likely to receive a much more sympathetic reading from my editor at HarperCollins. For that reason alone, I should have made more effort with the names of the characters in it.

But I'm a slow learner. And even when I'd stepped up to the present day, and was writing **Until Dawn Tomorrow**, (1995), a contemporary novel set in London in the mid-Nineties, couldn't I have come up with a better name for my alter-ego detective inspector than 'Frank Kavanagh'?

I suppose 'Frank' is just about all right, given his age (he's in his forties).

But 'Kavanagh'? What does that 'say'? Irish (ish) of course. But why did I do that? Shame-faced, I confess that I've absolutely no idea. What it *did* mean was that I then had to give him some (spurious) history that I only came up with because of the name that I had saddled him with.

OK, that kind of organic development can be fruitful, but I'm sure that, had I spent a bit of time thinking about a name for this character, it would have said something more, and more appropriate, for me.

(I wasn't to know, of course, that even as **Until Dawn Tomorrow** was being printed, ITV were creating the John Thaw vehicle, *Kavanagh QC,* a programme that would air at the same time as my book was published.

I doubt that my few thousand readers were going to suffer any confusion that they couldn't manage to read a book whose main character shared a name with a famous TV creation. And I suppose you could even make a case for saying that any reflection from the bigger pool of TV, plus John Thaw, could do no midlist writer any harm. But I'd still recommend avoiding confusion with other fictional characters if you possibly can.)

DI Frank Kavanagh's girlfriend, Jane *Salt*, is Jewish. Her family's name had been changed a generation previously from *Saltzman* – on account of the anti-Semitic prejudice that her father had encountered in this country. All very well, but unfortunately, I could never get excited about the name '*Jane Salt*', even though I like her character and enjoy writing her.

I think it was the combination of the monosyllabic 'Jane' with the equally unadorned 'Salt' that was the mistake there. Oh, well, I suppose they might get married? 'Jane *Kavanagh*'? (Not bad, actually!)

*

Personally, I like straightforward names like Patricia Highsmith's 'Tom Ripley'. It's neat, it's 'clean', and it writes well. There's no sense of artifice or 'baggage'. I don't care for Patricia Cornwell's 'Kay Scarpetta', or Sara Paretsky's 'VI Warshawski', which feel to me like made-up American names for sassy women.

I don't much care for Rankin's awkward (to my ear) 'John Rebus', nor the over-weeningly arch forename for Colin Dexter's creation, 'Endeavour' (Morse). Ruth Rendell's 'Wexford' sounds parochial, (which is fair enough) but 'Reg' now sounds rather old-fashioned.

If the evidence didn't contradict me, I'd also suggest avoiding those peculiarly English names/words, which three quarters of the population has no idea how to pronounce: Magdalen (an Oxford college) pronounced 'maudlin'; Belvoir (the Vale of, in Leicestershire) pronounced 'beaver'; Siobhan (pronounced 'shavawn').

But Reginald Hill has featured his popular detective Dalziel (pronounced 'dee-ell') for so long now that I must be wrong. Again.

PD James's 'Adam Dalgleish' strikes me as a fine name. Baroness James said recently that she had been taught English by a teacher of that name, and had probably subconsciously absorbed the name as a sort of homage to her teacher. More strangely, it later transpired that her teacher had been married to a man whose forename was 'Adam', something which she can hardly have known.

Personally, I have a wholly irrational prejudice against names that muddle the reader's notion of gender: 'Sam' for Samuel or Samantha; 'Jo' for Joseph or Josephine; 'Toni' and 'Chris'. Is any initial playful cross-gender ambiguity worth being lumbered with a confusingly-named character for the next three hundred pages?

*

I also have an antipathy towards characters with what appear to be two *fore*names. I'd therefore avoid handles like Eddie George (banker); Charlie George (ex-footballer); Susan George (actress), and Boy George (DJ); George Graham (football manager); George Michael (singer), George Thomas (House of Commons Speaker), and so on.

I would also suggest that you avoid calling your characters names that are similar to one another, or even begin with the same letter, simply to avoid unnecessary confusion for the reader.

Thomas Harris writes books that sell in millions, (**Silence of the Lambs,** 1988; **Hannibal,** 1999) and are sold to film-makers for millions of dollars more. So what do I know? And what right do I have to criticise Harris's methods. Nothing, and none, are the answers. So here goes.

In **Hannibal,** there's a '*Verger*', (he's not one, of course, any more than the character, '*Mason*' is a Mason). But there's also a '*Volmer*', and a '*Vellmore*'. Now, that's three names with two syllables beginning with the same (fairly unusual) letter.

Even if, in the polymorphous nation soup that is America, you really *can* find in the pages of the Baltimore phone directory a Vellmore, a Verger and a Volmer, is it a good idea for a writer to use such similar names in the same book?

Or is this – more likely – just one of those slips that writers make at the first-draft stage as they sashay from one idea to the next, one chapter to the next, carrying with them not only plot and ideas information, but a sort of DNA trace of previous characters' names that can, easily and subconsciously, soon get used again? I know I do this. But generally, by the third draft, and certainly by the editing stage, you hope that someone will have picked up these idiosyncrasies.

So, where *does* one go for names that are going to feel right, read right, and write right? I'd forget the most obvious source: the telephone directory, frankly, has simply too many entries.

If I see or hear an interesting name, on the news, in the papers, on TV, I often write it down. (Unfortunately, when I come to write the next book, I can rarely find the piece of paper that I've written it on.)

Of course, if you're going to use a person's name from 'life', either someone you know, or whose name has appeared in the media, check that you're within your legal rights to do so.

Jeffrey Archer apparently sometimes auctions the right of his friends to have their actual names used in his fiction. A sort of dubious fame/notoriety, I guess.

A wander round a churchyard is often good for names, too, even if a little depressing sometimes.

But personally, most often, in my trawl for names, I go to the football leagues. Any decent sports section of a Sunday newspaper gives the full team lists, and there's 92 clubs in the English League. That's a lot of – frequently changing – names. It's where I picked up Presley; Kilbane, Angel, and Kavanagh.

For minor characters, I might drop the odd mate or acquaintance's name in. Generally, a forename combined with a different surname. South London gangster 'Ray Annets' in **Small Vices**, was a *petit homage* to my chum Gus Annetts, famous in certain west London restaurants for his serviette-on-nose balancing trick. DI Tom Bromage in the same book was a mention of my builder chum, Dave Bromage, and a footballing mate, Tom.

But, as I say, be very careful that your acknowledgements of friends and acquaintance are not unwelcome, and don't associate evil-doing characters with the names of real people under any circumstances. I know when I heard that I shared my surname with an alleged paedophile during a recent media/vigilante witch-hunt,

I felt an uncomfortable frisson every time the man's name was even mentioned on TV.

Similarly, when striker 'David Armstrong' used to knock them in for Southampton FC a few years ago, my feelings of pleasure watching *Match of the Day* were always accompanied by a little unease. I imagined the guys I've played football with down the years who would be having a snigger as they thought of me, the clumsy left-back who couldn't head the ball for toffee, compared with his namesake down on the south coast who was popping them in for the Saints in his red and white stripes.

Tips and Summary:

1) If you don't do it, (write that book) you won't have to fret about names
2) Given that you probably *are* going to do it, choose a name for your hero that sits easy on the tongue and the page, and that you won't mind writing a few thousand times

OTHER JOBS ...

'... all trades, their gear and tackle and trim.
All things counter, original, spare, strange;'

Gerard Manley Hopkins *Pied Beauty*

Very few people leave school or university and start writing. Invariably they do something else first, and the something that many of them do is teach.

Novelist and TV screenwriter Andrew Davies was a college lecturer. DH Lawrence was a teacher, Anthony Burgess was an education officer in Malaya. David Lodge and Malcolm Bradbury were university lecturers, as is Manchester-based novelist, Richard Francis. The list is endless.

Is it the ready-made audience of students? Or is it the (supposedly) amenable conditions – a warm room, an endless supply of pens and stationery; long(ish) holidays, repeated exposure to the syllabus literature, and the relatively short working days?

But teaching is only one of many professions followed by writers: Philip Larkin was a librarian; Richard Gordon (the **Doctor** series of novels) was a surgeon; Douglas Hurd, Edwina Currie, Julian Critchley and Benjamin Disraeli were all politicians first, writers second.

Richard Adams (**Watership Down**) was in the civil service. Ian Fleming was Director of Naval Intelligence; Henry Fielding was a Justice of the Peace, and author of **Tristram Shandy,** Laurence Sterne, a vicar.

Dirk Bogarde and Joan Collins were both successful actors; and there seems to be a fashion for comedians (Ben Elton; Alexei Sayle; David Baddiel, Rob Newman, Stephen Fry and Hugh Laurie) to metamorphose into novelists.

There are journalists aplenty, from Julie Burchill and Hunter Davies to Paul Eddy, and TV presenters like Gerald Seymour, Alan Titchmarsh and, most recently, with **Stripped Bare**, 2003, Lowri Turner.

The advertising industry lost to fiction Fay Weldon, Michael Dobbs and James Herbert.

When I left school, I worked in a shop that sold wallpaper and paint. Subsequently I was a van driver, builder, door-to-door salesman, ice-cream delivery man, and worked in the cut glass department at House of Fraser.

I eventually went to college and university and then taught English for a good few years while trying to write.

There were happy times teaching, good colleagues and pleasant students whom it was a pleasure to work with. And teaching English literature is probably no bad thing for a writer (as long as it doesn't completely inhibit one's own faltering attempts).

But, honestly, when I think of the times I was most happy in my life, it was probably when, as a young man, I was living in a squat in Cheltenham with a few dope-smoking hippy friends, and working for a local butcher a couple of hours a day delivering pork chops to elderly ladies and hotel kitchens.

Mindless work, youth, and a nice environment amongst friends. Yes, the sun did seem to shine, and *Sergeant Pepper* seemed to be the soundtrack to our lives. Of course it may well, in reality, have all been a bit fey and fake, but the pleasant memory abides.

Many years later, after I'd published four novels and just had the new one turned down, I even tried to recapture a bit of that time and spirit.

I was living with my girlfriend in Manchester and, instead of registering to do some twenty-five pounds per hour supply teaching or putting myself about on the writers' circuit (I'd lost confidence, with the new book having been rejected, anyway) I took a job with a big car dealership delivering their new vehicles to customers, collecting them for service, or delivering stock to other branches.

It was a part-time job. They'd give me a call when there was a car to be taken out or picked up from somewhere. The pay was about five pounds an hour and my Manchester geography was non-existent. I'd set off in some brand new saloon to go to Stockport (twenty minutes away) and return, four hours later.

I didn't stay long, even though they were really pretty understanding about my longish delivery trips. There was no *Sergeant Pepper* on the car stereo and the sun didn't shine much.

It wasn't very long before I sat down again, and started writing.

Tips and Summary:

1) Don't do it
2) Especially when you are young, do as wide a variety of jobs as you can. They'll often be low paid and involve long hours and tedium. Perfect for fostering the writing spirit.
3) Lots of writers have been teachers, but that environment doesn't work for everyone.

'Madam, a circulating library in a town is an evergreen tree of diabolical knowledge!'

Richard Brinsley Sheridan, *The Rivals*

There are very few joys in the midlist writer's life, but PLR is probably one of them.

PLR is not the 'red' petrol you put in older motor cars – that's LRP – PLR is Public Lending Right: every time a reader borrows a book from a library in this country, some sort of electronic register records the fact, and boosts that writer's earnings by 4 pence. Not bad, eh?

The scheme was set up in 1979, the result of a prolonged campaign by writers Brigid Brophy, Maureen Duffy, Lady Antonia Fraser and others, and politicians Lord Ted Willis in the House of Lords, Norman St John Stevas, and the late Labour Party leader, John Smith, in the House of Commons.

The thinking behind the idea was this: books are bought by libraries to be read by a wide public at no cost to the reader. An admirable enterprise, of course. But what about the writer? It takes most of us the best part of a year to complete a novel. OK, John Creasey often used to knock them out in less than a month, and we know that Georges Simenon wrote some of his – pretty good – short novels in even less time than that. But for most of us, it's a time-consuming business and, along with paying the bills and doing the shopping, by the time we've trawled through several drafts, gone down blind alleys as we sort out the niceties of plot and characters, the whole thing takes something like a year.

Publishers print about a thousand or fifteen hundred copies of little-known (genre) writers, often in the reasonable expectation that they might sell a good number of this run – depending upon reviews, the librarian's taste, and familiarity with the author's previous titles – to libraries. This is sufficient to put the print run into profit against the advance that has been paid to the writer and the other expenses involved in publishing a book.

And while it's true that many midlist writers would, without these library purchases, sell very few hardback copies – the cost, often seventeen or eighteen pounds, being prohibitive – even in this commercial two-way street, was it fair that the writers of these books should not benefit further from their titles being repeatedly loaned out?

The 1979 Public Lending Right scheme, funded by the government to the tune of £4.5 million to 2002 (and increased to £6.2 million in 2003) was designed to address this very issue. Given that 75% of authors earn less than *half* of the national average wage for their efforts, it was clearly needed.

The money is apportioned in a democratic way: there is a ceiling of £6,000, no matter how successful the author. This is to preclude Catherine Cookson and Jeffrey Archer having *all* the available money.

At the other end of the spectrum, the author of **Polymer Fabrics for Everyday Yacht Applications** receives the minimum cheque (for £5) if *his* life's work is borrowed just a couple of hundred times.

When I gave up being a lecturer (in 1993) I was earning about £22,000 a year, pre-tax. Since that time I have not earned enough money from my writing to have paid a tax bill. Not once.

I have five novels in print, four of them in large print editions, three of them available on audio, and even a translation or two. I've had two plays performed, quite a bit of journalism published and do several talks and workshops each year, but I'm still not in the tax bracket.

172

It's for these reasons that February's PLR cheque is so welcome to most midlist writers.

The first year that I was eligible for a payment (the calculations are done to June of the previous year, and are based on a representative sample of four hundred libraries throughout the country) was 1994, a year after **Night's Black Agents** had been published. The cheque was for £150. Given my earnings, £150 was welcome. But even more gratifying than the cheque was the fact that, there in black and white, was evidence that some seven and a half thousand people had already borrowed my book.

By the following year, thirteen thousand more readers had borrowed **Night's Black Agents**, and another eight thousand, the new one, **Less Than Kind**. The cheque was for over £400.

By 1997, and with three titles available, my PLR cheque was just short of a thousand pounds, which represented borrowings of about forty-three thousand. Not bad – that's a three-quarters full Old Trafford, or more than the population of the town where I live. It was ... a lot of people.

But everything's relative: as I've said, I've never yet seen anyone reading one of my books on the bus or a park bench. (My London-based son did claim that he had once seen someone walking down the road with a copy of **Night's Black Agents** under his arm, but he is a very nice son.)

In any event, forty-three thousand was a satisfyingly chunky number, and here was my cheque to prove it. Excellent. *Only accrue.*

Since that time, payments have hovered around the twelve or thirteen hundred pound mark. But the sobering fact is, no matter how devoted your readers are, they can't be expected to read your existing titles repeatedly and, unless you get a new one onto the shelf every year or so, your loan figures will very quickly slip.

Just as it was a long and acrimonious battle to get the scheme through parliament and on to the statute book, with ministers such as Ian Sproate and Douglas Hurd (himself a writer of thrillers) both hostile to the idea of PLR, there have sometimes been dark mutterings about the scheme's being abandoned. But the opposition seems not to have reared its head for a while now so, hopefully, this welcome source of much-needed revenue will continue for the future.

As a writer, when you go to a library, there's something very pleasing about seeing your titles ranged along the shelf there. (Of course, it's much better if they're *not* there, as long as you can assume that they are not there because they are out on loan, and being read.)

What is depressing, though, is that sometimes they are not there because one of your readers has *stolen* the book rather than merely borrowed it. Not only has this person deprived every other reader of the opportunity to read your book, but there will now be no more stamps in the leaf of the title, and if, as must surely sometimes happen, this is one of the branches that is taking part in the survey of loans on which PLR calculations are made, you are going to lose a chunk of your income.

Please don't steal library books. Or at least, don't steal *mine*!

One 'reader' opted not to steal my local library's copy of **Until Dawn Tomorrow**, and instead, with the passion of a zealot and the pen of a psychopath (thick, smudgy blue biro) deleted every single swear word that had offended him/her.

Given that it is a crime novel, set in contemporary London and the Midlands, there was, necessarily, some 'bad' language. I was sorry to see the book defaced in this way. The novel is now out of print and no longer available. The only copy that the library has, will, no doubt, at the next library sale, finds its way into the 10p box and my library borrowings and PLR payments will plummet, alas!

Tips and Summary:

1) Don't write that book, and leave the rest of us to share the available money.

2) Register your books at the earliest possible time.

3) Get friends and family, from Stornoway to Land's End, to request your books at their local libraries.

4) As a midlist writer, you *have* to accrue. It's unlikely that you'll have one huge hit, rather, it's a translation here, an audio deal there, a large print edition, and a bit of PLR that will, (just about) keep you afloat.

5) Most importantly, for yourself, for your publisher *and* for your PLR, keep the books coming. Keep up the work-rate so that, (without impairing the quality of your output) you come up with the goods: a new book every year or so.

QUOTATIONS

'I often quote myself. It adds spice to my conversation.'

GB Shaw

When I used to teach, I'd say to my A-level students to think of their own words as the bricks, and a line or two from the author they were studying as the *cement* that would bind those bricks to make a good wall.

If you're going to use quotations in *your* novel, they need to be apt, to 'fall trippingly from the tongue'. You don't want them to stand out as if they are there merely to display your precocious learning.

But mostly, of course, it's for book titles that writers seek out an appropriate and pithy quotation. And if you hit on something succinct that also represents the theme or essence of your novel, it's a bonus.

Writing in the *Observer* recently, Robert McCrum suggested to readers that while a decent book is likely to sell, irrespective of the title, Margaret Mitchell was probably well advised to change her original choice of **Ba Ba Blacksheep** to the rather more resonant **Gone With The Wind.**

Similarly, Robert Louis Stevenson was surely better served by **Treasure Island** than the rather prosaic **The Sea Cook**. McCrum also mentions that we might have been calling those intractable dilemmas that we all occasionally face **Catch 19**, rather than **22**, had Joseph Heller stuck with his original idea.

While I was writing my first book, I called it **The Narrowboat Murders**. Why not? It was set on the waterways around Birmingham and the killer was a boatman. **The Narrowboat Murders** was fair enough.

I'd had an interrupted and unhappy education, only going to

177

university when I was 23. My good friend Penny had had a proper, sixth-form Cheltenham girls' school education, and knew her Shakespeare (which, along with the Bible, of course, is the source of most book titles).

When she read the book, she suggested three words from **Macbeth**: *Good things of day begin to droop and drowse as **night's black agents** to their preys do rouse.*

I was grateful to her for this atmospheric title that at once fitted the dark and claustrophobic nature of the story, and also gave it the cachet that my own pedestrian title did not.

I don't think it matters whether the title reflects very accurately the content of the book, it's more a question of conveying the atmosphere.

After all, is **Angela's Ashes** what Frank McCourt's bestseller is really *about*?

Isn't the episode in Thomas Harris's **Silence of the Lambs**, where the fetching title is alluded to, no more than a bit of spurious, cod-psychology that's grafted on to the Clarice Starling character's past, and doesn't really bear examination?

And while Captain Corelli's mandolin *does* play a charming part in Louis de Bernieres's wonderful book of that title, it's hardly seminal.

By the time I was writing the second book, my title antennae were out there and quivering. One of the book's main springs of action is the double-dealing and infidelity within a wealthy country family.

I knew Hamlet pretty well and the line, '*A little more than kith and **less than kind**'* was an absolute gift for the book.

There's no copyright in titles, but it's a good idea to go along and check **Books in Print** in your local library to ascertain whether anyone else has used your proposed title recently, simply to avoid confusion when your book is published.

The other place to check is when you (or your publisher,)

register the book for its ISBN (International Society of Book Numbering).

Ignoring my own advice, I didn't do either of these things when I came up with the title for my most recent book.

I'd always loved the lines, spoken by Gloucester in **King Lear**: *'Through tatter'd clothes, small vices do appear/robes and furr'd gowns hide all.'*

As a matter of fact, unknown to me, the American writer Robert Parker had got there before me (with *his* **Small Vices**, published by No Exit Press in 1999). But the quotation itself, and the words **Small Vices** in particular, were so absolutely right for the theme of my book – people in high office getting away with dodgy dealings, while the indigent get banged up or bumped off – that I used it anyway. And after all, the title had only been used for a relatively little-known book (certainly in this country).

Small Vices was a return to Shakespeare. In books three and four, I'd been elsewhere for my titles. The third book, **Until Dawn Tomorrow**, was the first of my books to be set at a contemporary time (1995), and I wanted it to have an up-to-date feel.

At that time, at 8.56 every morning on Radio Four you'd hear: 'And now the weather forecast for the United Kingdom, *until dawn tomorrow.*' There was my title.

Thought For The Day, my fourth book, is set around an advertising agency, and a lot of it takes place in London. Again, I wanted a contemporary feel, and so opted for the four words which epitomise for me the idiosyncratic nature of the media in general, and one of Radio Four's charms in particular: the odd notion in our (largely) secular world, of people as diverse as Rabbi Lionel Blue, Buddhist, Satash Kumar, and the Bishop of Oxford sharing their spiritual/world view with us while we make our toast and coffee.

So, for your title, read Shakespeare, and read the Bible. But get there quickly; they've been plundered often, and those pithy titles can't last for ever.

Tips and Summary:

1) If you don't write your book, you can stick to reading for pleasure, not with half an eye on the title for your next book in Shakespeare, the classics and the Bible.
2) If you insist on writing it, visit the above for your title

READING ALOUD

'She reads at such a pace,' she explained, 'and when I asked her where she had learnt to read so quickly, she replied, "On the screens at cinemas."'

Ronald Firbank

Reading work aloud is absolutely essential. There's something about hearing the words you've written, not merely within the confines of your imagination – in your head – but out in the air. Hearing them in this way helps you to tell whether all sorts of things are working – or not.

When you hear a passage of dialogue, even if the exchanges are pretty snappy and short (which I'd recommend generally, anyway) you can hear whether this is the way that people do (apparently) actually speak. I say apparently, because to commit *actual* speech to the page would be dull and irritating: most of us use far too many ums and ahs, and all sorts of hesitations and verbal tics.

The art, as a writer, is to render something which has the *rhythm* of speech, and which sounds like the exchanges that people *do* have, but to omit those tics and repetitions.

Think of those 1940's movies where Humphrey Bogart snaps out a line, only for Katherine Hepburn to reply with a pithy riposte. It's not like that in real life – people are rarely that bright and quick.

I've spent my adult life hoping to have exchanges of the sort that I hear in black and white movies on Sunday afternoons, only to be disappointed to find that my own conversations are made up of the platitudes and hiatus of mortals, rather than the seamless, sparky banter that has been honed by a team of Hollywood script-writers.

But it's not only dialogue that benefits from reading aloud. It's

181

every bit as true for descriptive passages. Reading work aloud, you hear the pace and the tone of what you have written in a way that is entirely different from any 'internal' reading, and this will help you pick up redundancies and repetitions, and spot omissions in sound or sense.

So, when you are working on your novel, and you have written a reasonable chunk of material, give the work a day or two to 'settle', and then try reading it out loud.

There *will* be occasions when the prose reads flat or lumpy, the dialogue unconvincing and forced, and you might only be able to salvage a few paragraphs from half a dozen pages.

But there will be other times when you will find yourself pleasantly surprised. A sort of, 'Gosh, did I *really* write that?

Many writers enjoy writing dialogue, but the danger is that *you* are enjoying writing it rather more than your readers are going to savour reading it. The very fact that the words come easily, and that you've done half a dozen pages of work in little time, should signal danger.

Do we need to hear this? Is it slowing down the story without adding much to it?

The case for verisimilitude might decree that characters chat, but this is art, not life, and it's invariably the shorter, tighter version of your book that will carry the punch, not the flabby, self-indulgent one.

It's a fact that some writers just don't do dialogue well. Thomas Hardy, so able at evoking character and place, frequently has a completely wooden ear for conversation, forcing chunks of unsayable 'dialogue' into the mouths of his characters.

Some of the things that he has Jude Fawley utter in **Jude the Obscure** are obviously not that character 'speaking', but merely stuttering expressions of the author's philosophy. Admittedly, Hardy

182

was writing his fiction in the nineteenth century, and language and speech patterns have changed, but I don't think you need to have been at a place, and at a time, to recognise proselytising that is masquerading as dialogue.

It seems almost unfair to refer to the 'speech' that Jeffrey Archer gives his characters to say. Suffice to say that the dialogue in **Sons of Fortune** (2003) the *Sunday Times's* reviewer felt 'resembled nothing so much as some peculiarly stilted language tapes: "Good evening, Mrs Coulter, how nice to meet you and your husband, and this must be your daughter Diane, if I remember correctly.""

Thriller writer Gerald Seymour (**A Line in the Sand,** 1999), tries his dialogue out on his dogs when he walks them each morning, but even if you're stuck in your study, there's a bonus to reading your prose aloud – it's perfect practice for when you read your work in public.

I have sat through some truly terrible readings. Some writers seem to feel that it is enough for them to turn up at a bookshop or library and mumble inaudibly through a few pages of their new book.

One novelist wrote in the crime writers' trade magazine, *Red Herrings*, a while ago, that we should all go on public speaking courses before signing up to give readings. This may be taking things a bit far, but I do think that we should practise before we inflict ourselves on readers.

Audiences at book-signings, launches, readers' groups and work-shops won't expect a RADA-trained actor's delivery, but the ability to convey the flavour of your work successfully is obviously of great benefit.

And don't forget, although *you* are familiar with the piece that you are reading, your listeners are hearing it for the first time. I often find it's worth photocopying for the audience the couple of pages I am reading. It helps to make them feel 'included', and it certainly aids their understanding to see, as well as hear, the words being read.

Whenever you're invited to do a talk or a workshop or reading, accept the offer, even if you're nervous about your own ability. It's good practice, and if you rehearse it a few times in your own sitting room, you'll get better. It's the only way. You might even get to enjoy it.

Sometimes, book written and published, a producer will want an author to read his or her own stuff for audio-tape, CD, or radio.

Alain de Botton has recently read his **The Art of Travel** on Radio Four.

Some writers' work is indivisible from their own delivery, so familiar are we with their distinctive readings. Garrison Keillor's tales of the residents of Lake Wobegon – which themselves began as radio show contributions in the far north west of the USA – led to eventual publication and huge book sales in the 1980's. Bill Bryson's accounts of his travels through England and the USA are inextricably linked with the writer's voice; and is it conceivable to imagine Alan Bennett's work being read by anyone other than the author himself?

For midlist writers, though, a producer will invariably recruit a professional for the work. My own **Night's Black Agents** was read for audio by ex-*EastEnders* actor, Michael Tudor Barnes; **Until Dawn Tomorrow** was read by Christopher Kay, and **Thought For the Day** by Hayward Morse.

But in autumn of 2001, I did read some of my own work on Radio Four's arts programme, *Front Row*. The piece (about the misery for midlist writers of visiting bookshops, a version of which is reproduced in this book) was so personal, that I think the producer thought it would be better coming from the author rather than from a professional actor.

I was nervous, recording something just before it went out on national radio, but I was glad to be given the opportunity to do it.

Tips and summary:

1) Every few days, give your work a read-through – aloud.
2) Keep dialogue short, snappy and involving.
3) Beware of writing too much dialogue: it can be deceptively easy to write.
4) Try to give each of your characters a distinctive 'voice'.
5) Practice, so that you are at ease reading your work in public.
6) Always accept offers to give readings and do talks: it's good for the bank balance, and it's good to see what works (or doesn't) in front of an audience.

RESEARCH

'I researched my book on jazz by wandering around New York out of it with my Walkman on.'

Geoff Dyer

As a writer, the fourth question that you are frequently asked is: Do you have to do much research? (The first three are: Where do you get your ideas from? *Almost anywhere except from people at parties who tell you they have a great idea for a book.* Do you have to be disciplined? *Yes.* And, How long does it take you to write a book? *Depends on the book, how much time you put in on it, and how many snags you face: John Creasey, two days; Georges Simenon, two weeks; James Thackeray, twenty years. Most writers take about a year to complete a novel.*)

Most of us don't write the sort of books that Jack Higgins and Fredcrick Forsyth do, with lots of detail about the calibre of pistols and the speed and controls of fighter jets.

But certainly, people *do* like to read about 'things', to learn about 'stuff', about people's trades and their occupations.

There are any number of writers who specialise in one area of knowledge and expertise, from Dick Francis's horse-racing thrillers, to Michael Dobbs's political novels, James Herriot's veterinary-set books, and the sea-faring works of Patrick O'Brien.

And in recent years, there's been a penchant for specific treatments of one narrow area of interest: Dava Sobel's **Longitude** (1995); Deborah Moggach's **Tulip Fever** (2000) and Joanne Harris's **Chocolat** (1998).

But in generic novels (crime, for example) you have to go very easy on the amount of information you offer to the reader if you are to integrate it seamlessly into the story.

It *is* exciting to read about how Frederick Forsyth's 'Jackal' assembles his wares, changes his appearance, and cleverly acquires a false identity from a graveyard tombstone, but it takes a lot of skill to integrate this sort of information into the text without it looking forced and lumpy. Too much research, if it's on the *page*, rather than in the writer's mind, can really stifle a book.

Historical novelist Rosalind Miles (**Guenevere: Queen of the Summer Country,** 1999) says that it takes her five years to research a book, but only a year to write it, and that there can be a temptation to use too much of the material that she has gathered.

Certain novels, of course, are absolutely knitted to the subject that the author has painstakingly researched. Thomas Kenneally might have been inspired to tell the story of Oscar Schindler (**Schindler's Ark,** 1986) after visiting a luggage store in California, but he then had to research the whole period, the part that Schindler had played in the story, and interview any survivors or their relatives.

Robert Harris's **Enigma** (1995), and **Fatherland** (1992), similarly, are the outcome of very detailed historical research wedded to the novelist's conjecture: What if…?

*

I don't have to read up in this way to write my books. The novels that I have published are more about people and relationships, than *things*. But in **Until Dawn Tomorrow**, when a cop states that three dozen corpses are pulled from the River Thames each year, or in **Small Vices**, that pylons carry some 400,000 volts of electricity, you owe it to your readers to try and make sure that the information is correct.

When I'm writing, and need to check details of this sort, I tend to simply leave a gap and a question mark in the text and subsequently make the enquiries, for the simple reason that the writing is both the hardest and the best part of the day. It might be tough, but it's exciting and exhilarating, too.

Even when you're tired and written-out, you can make a telephone call, send an e-mail, or write a letter.

I can find out about Thames' corpses and electricity pylons later, but I might *not* be able to hit the writing rhythm, so if that's going well, I always stick with it.

The internet (supposedly) is the contemporary writer's greatest repository of information and research tool. I'm sure it is, but, Oh dear, do *I* have problems with it! To take only one example, in writing this book about writing, I wanted to check how many publishers had turned down **The Day of the Jackal** before it found a publisher (and went on to become the huge bestseller it is).

I typed in 'Frederick Forsyth' and '**The Day of the Jackal**'. The search engine came up with 940 sites. Nine hundred and *forty*. I could have spent all day looking for the snippet I needed. And that was for an inconsequential (but important) line in an early chapter. The problem with the internet, as many users find, is that there is just too *much* information there.

My pre-internet research experiences have been mixed, too. Of course, I use libraries and librarians for all sorts of information. I've found with them – just as I've found with all the other people I've ever met – that some of them are helpful and kind, friendly and interested, and some of them are miserable and awkward, taciturn and unfriendly.

I've been invited to do talks and workshops in several branch libraries, and many of them have indicated a willing enthusiasm to stock my books. But I've also met with sniffy and supercilious librarians, who seem unable to connect the person standing at their enquiry desk with the books that weigh down their shelves.

As a published writer, you are entitled to join the British Library in St Pancras. It's a beautiful building and it has a good book and audio shop, cafés, and an open roof space. But, best of all, you can work there, take your laptop, or merely a pad and pen, and access any one of their millions of volumes. It's a wonderful place.

If you want to visit the beautiful domed reading room, beloved of any number of writers and scholars for many years, go to the old British Library in Russell Square.

Colindale newspaper library in north London is a great resource if you're trying to find specific information from a particular date or, indeed, if you want to get accurate background to events of a particular time.

In writing five novels during the last eight or nine years, I've had to track down any number of bits of idiosyncratic information. Trouble is, very often, the kind of thing that you need to know can sound absurdly inconsequential. At the worst, librarians (or others) assume that you are trying to find out the answer to something to win a tenner in the local pub general knowledge quiz.

Back in 1996, writing **Thought For the Day**, I needed a plausible back-story for one of the characters, a villain called Kenny Angel. Angel was running a slightly dodgy security firm in the 1980s. He was an ex-soldier who had been drummed out of the army and drifted into this barely-legal 'security' work, supposedly protecting people and their assets.

My ex-soldier needed to have been serving abroad in the mid- to late-1970s. Where *were* British troops serving, and with which regiments, at that time? I telephoned the Ministry of Defence.

Newscaster-turned-writer Gerald Seymour says, 'You can't write a contemporary thriller from newspaper cuttings, but as a novelist doing research, you have no status, so your line of patter has to work.'

The MOD sent me to some Army information number (that

was in fact, for recruitment). From there, I was routed to the Imperial War Museum (unlikely, I thought, but who knows) and from there to a couple of other Whitehall numbers. Maybe they thought I was nuts.

Anyway, after five or six long-distance calls, and being shunted from one department and office to another, I eventually got through to a Major somewhere who was said to be dealing with public relations.

I'm from Birmingham, and as anyone who comes from that city knows, the accent's as good as a written undertaking that you will not be taken seriously by anyone, anywhere, in the entire rest of the UK.

The Major listened to my enquiry, took a deep, ex-Sandhurst breath and said, in a Majorly-plummy dismissive voice: 'It sounds to me as if you want *me* to do your research for you.'

Several phone calls, a deal of time and a little money, to draw a complete blank on a mere detail for one character's back-story.

Oh, well, as Tama Janowitz (**A Certain Age**, 1999) says: 'Writing is getting used to being humiliated.'

I'm sure if you are Lynda LaPlante, you can call up an East-End gangster and be down at the Blind Beggar pub and hobnobbing with any number of villains who will share their dodgy exploits with you in a flash. If Patricia Cornwell needs to sit in at the morgue to brush up her autopsy skills; if Ian Rankin wants to check out the basement of the Scottish parliament; or Martina Cole wants to ride shotgun through Stoke Newington with the drugs squad, I doubt they will face much of a problem.

However, if you are a midlist writer, the response may not be quite so helpful.

In the mid-1990s, setting a scene from **Until Dawn Tomorrow** in the BBC TV *Crimewatch* studio, I wrote to the producer and asked if I could observe the studio to get the details right. There are literally dozens of people there, lots of cops and presenters, (including Nick Ross and, at the time, the late Jill Dando). One more person, sitting out of the way somewhere...

The answer, of course, was a polite *No*. I think if I'd been Ruth Rendell or Ian Rankin ...

So, yes, even for essentially non-technical crime novels, where the main focus is not the calibre of the bullet, the trajectory of the missile, or the length of the detonating fuse, there's still a lot of incidental detail that you need to get right for obvious professional reasons. And if you don't, one of your readers will very quickly let you know.

When I have a character in **Night's Black Agents** – set in Birmingham in the 1930s – supping a pint of Mitchell's and Butler's Mild ale, I should have checked, rather than simply assumed that 'Mild' was for sale then. A reader at a subsequent signing session could not contain his quietly-spoken glee. Two hundred pages, eighty thousand words, but he'd spotted the error.

Fair enough, I suppose: you can't hope for attentive readers, *and* then criticise them for ultra-careful reading.

Tips and Summary:

1) For most novels, put the writing first, you can do 'research' at any time.

2) Don't swamp the reader with a lot of information just because you've painstakingly gathered it.

3) No one buys a book for the research.

4) Try and get things right. Check, and then check again; in particular, things that you are simply making familiar assumptions about – you'll be surprised how often you'll be wrong.

5) Be polite and friendly in making your enquiries.

6) Enjoy research. It isn't really work, but it feels like it. You get to wander around with a pad and pen and your specs on looking studious. You even feel like you might actually *be* a writer.

REVIEWS

'I find that even a favourable notice makes me feel sick nowa-days, while an unfavourable one, even from a small provincial newspaper, puts me off my work for days.'

PG Wodehouse

I've been pretty fortunate with my reviews. There was one snooty jibe from Gerald Kaufman in the north London *Ham and High* for **Thought For The Day**: '40 pages from the end, a new character is introduced and, sadly, the whole story disintegrates', (a 'fact' which, incidentally, isn't true). But that was very much the exception, and the MP does have a penchant for a rather weaselly tone. I remember seeing a review of his of one of Tory MP, Julian Critchley's, books which was mean-spirited beyond reason. I actually took the time to write to Critchley – all of this was *before* I had received Kaufman's opprobrium, so there was no 'agenda' on my side. The late Critchley's reply to me was sanguine about his political foe.

But, generally, the notices for my novels have been pretty good, and only more modesty than I possess would preclude my citing critic Philip Oakes. Writing in the *Literary Review,* he referred to **Night's Black Agents** as, 'a tale of crime and punishment that Zola would not disown'.

John Coleman in the *Sunday Times* called **Until Dawn Tomorrow**, 'Unequivocally excellent,' and Donna Leon, writing in the same paper, said of **Thought For The Day** that it was, 'bleak and brilliant'.

By any standards, these are tasty cuttings for the folder. Why, then, is it the dismissive Kaufman, with his one paragraph in the *Ham and High*, that I remember so clearly?

Worse, *why*, when **Until Dawn Tomorrow** is reviewed warmly in the *Financial Times, Daily Telegraph, The Times, Literary Review, New Law Journal*, and the *Guardian*, do my thoughts repeatedly return to the few words of harsh criticism penned in the *Sheffield Messenger* by some cub reporter?

*

Oddly, what can be just as mystifying and irritating as a hostile review, is the non-appearance of reviews of your book at all.

After all, newspapers need copy; bigger newspapers need even more copy, and that's why the broadsheets have pages of book reviews. But even these reviews represent only a small proportion of the books received by the literary editor of a newspaper from publicity-hungry publishers.

A writer-friend who reviews crime for one of the Sunday broadsheets told me recently that he receives five or six books each *day*, but that he has space for only five per *month* on the books pages.

But apart from the simple question of pressure on space, if your book fails to appear, what else might have happened? Has the reviewer moved on? Died? Been sacked?

Has the publisher's publicity person not sent the book to this or that newspaper? Has it been culled by a magazine editor who wants only the work of very well-known writers to be reviewed, irrespective of the merits of their work? Or has it just been over-looked and is, even now, languishing in the corner of the literary editor's office somewhere?

So mystified was I by the dearth of reviews of **Small Vices**, my last book, that I took the unusual step of contacting a couple of novelist friends who moonlight as reviewers. (It's not the first time I've contacted a reviewer: after Philip Oakes had reviewed **Thought For The Day** in the *Literary Review*, ending his notice with the words, '*British crime writing is on a roll at the moment, and*

194

this is about as good as it gets,' I felt it would be churlish not to acknowledge his comments.

I wrote to him, said that I was aware that I was probably contravening literary etiquette etc. but wanted to thank him. He wrote back, said forget etiquette, it was nice to hear, and that he enjoyed my books enormously and was looking forward to the next one.)

The first critic I contacted said she had received the book, and yes, she had enjoyed it, but her editor wanted only high-profile names on the page. (Of course, she *may* have been lying, embarrassed at my contacting her, but I don't think so.)

When I contacted another critic, she e-mailed me to say that she had not received her copy of the book.

There are *so* many cock-ups of this sort that, although it's very difficult to do these things for yourself, you might be wise to enquire what is going on. Yes, you risk being humiliated, told to mind your own business and not be so pushy. But my curiosity was so great, that it won out over even these deterrents. Just be polite, and remember: no one cares about your book and its fate more than you do.

No reviews; bad reviews; it doesn't even end there. For genre writers, there is another constant irritant. Get a few crime writers together and they will wail and moan about 'mainstream' writers getting half-page notices, while we get bunched together in some kind of job lot, with half a dozen books dispatched at once, just a couple of paragraphs to each.

Well, yes, maybe. But isn't it better to have this corralling of crime fiction every couple of weeks, than to be ignored completely?

However, the argument persists that our titles should have the same space as any other (i.e. 'literary') fiction. Well, actually, science fiction, romance and several other genres are generally much less extensively reviewed than crime.

And I know it's a hanging offence to say as much, but the crime novels I read – with a very few exceptions – simply don't warrant such attention. Is anyone going to seriously suggest that a book by Patricia Cornwell or even the great Elmore Leonard really demands the same kind of scrutiny as a novel by Jonathan Franzen or JM Coetzee?

Fact is, reviews might be good for the author ('thank God, I exist!') and good for the reviewer – he gets paid *and* gets a book for his shelf (or to flog to some dodgy dealer) – but I'm not convinced that it's reviews that sell many books.

In the case of well-known authors, a review might alert a reader to a writer's new book being available. But this assumes that potential readers have missed the other media exposure, the radio or TV appearances, the features in magazines and newspapers, the media hub-bub that accompanies a new Jeffrey Archer or Irvine Welsh.

But a poor review of an established writer doesn't, I believe, do much damage to sales. Tony Parsons's **Man and Wife** (2002) was slated in the press as being virtually a re-tread of his previous best-seller, **Man and Boy** (1999), (which was itself widely traduced).

The opening line of Peter Kemp's *Sunday Times* review declared: '*It's rare to encounter a novel quite as imaginatively poverty-stricken as* **Man and Wife**.' He goes on to tell would-be readers that the novel is '*narrated with mawkish garrulity*,' adds that the book '*resembles a plateful of stale second helpings*,' before concluding that Parsons has '*pioneered a new genre: Mills and Goon.*'

Parsons probably wasn't too upset by these harsh words. **Man and Boy** had been a bestseller, and by September 2002 **Man and Wife** was top of the hardback fiction charts having sold over twenty-six thousand copies within a month of publication.

Ben Elton's **High Society** (2002) the plot of which the *Sunday Times's* Adam Lively suggested had the '*meticulous implausibility of* *a Heath Robinson cartoon ...the characterisation not so much broadbrush as slapped on with a roller,'* sold eight thousand in hardback in its first fortnight on sale. The same writer's **Dead Famous** (2002), after eight weeks in the charts, had sold two hundred thousand in paperback.

Jeffrey Archer's **Sons of Fortune** (2003) 'Twin brothers, separated at birth, but fated to become rivals,' (sound familiar?) has, according to the *Sunday Times's* Joan Smith, *'uninspired prose... endless repetitions, improbable coincidences and limited emotional range,'* but if these features of Archer's work inhibit sales, it'll be the first time.

American Dave Pelzer's trio of books about the childhood abuse that he suffered, and his subsequent life, **A Child Called 'It'; A Man Named Dave**, and **The Lost Boy,** were generally scorned by reviewers, but all made the bestseller paperback list (often all three titles appearing together) and have sold in excess of one and a half million copies in Britain alone.

Iain Banks's **Dead Air** (2002), being described by Peter Parker in the *Sunday Times* as *'ill-disciplined and far too long,'* didn't stop Banks's readers buying nearly ten thousand hardbacks within four weeks of publication.

And it's not just writers at the popular end of the spectrum whose sales appear to be unaffected by the vitriol of poor reviews.

Former Booker Prize winner Ben Okri, (**The Famished Road**, 1991) was described by Alfred Hickling in the *Guardian* as making *'observations of staggering banality,'* in his more recent novel, **In Arcadia** (2002), while Will Self's **Dorian** (2002) was described by Tom Deveson in the *Sunday Times* as having shoddy prose and a poverty of wit, his writing being *'lazy and self-admiring'*. Have sales of these authors' books been dented by these notices? I rather doubt it.

The fact is, by the time that most popular authors have built up a decent readership, little can stop their forward momentum: you'd need to be unsighted not to be aware of the mediocre reviews that recent Patricia Cornwells have attracted, and reviews of Dick Francis's novels have been lukewarm for years now.

Quoting the devil for my own ends, Gerald Kaufman wrote of Francis's 1997 **10lb Penalty**, '... *fans will do their favourite author a favour by ignoring what is almost certainly the worst book he has written.*' But the horse-racing writer still kept producing a new novel each October, and his devoted readers bought it for their partner's Christmas stocking in the same way that my daughter puts a bag of Liquorice Allsorts in mine.

Novelist Simon Brett chose his words very carefully in reviewing Ian Rankin's **Resurrection Men** for the *Daily Mail* in January of 2002, but with phrases like '*Rebus is a somewhat reduced figure,*' and '*writers run out of things for the central character to do,*' there was no disguising his lack of enthusiasm for the Scotsman's latest novel.

I doubt that Brett's review lost Ian Rankin a single reader. With his faithful following, a career hiccup (if that's what it is) is unlikely to dislodge him from the position he currently holds.

These writers are like ocean-going oil tankers, whose forward progress takes a very long time to halt. The momentum of past sales ensures that their new work will invariably steam safely into port for some time to come.

Brian MacArthur, writing in *The Times* at the end of 2002, noted that, 'Once authors achieve an established reputation as bestsellers their success is repeated year after year...success breeds success.'

But anyway, even if readers ever feel disappointed enough that they actually choose not to buy the next title, the ancillary rights of the previous book will have been sold, the audio, TV and even film version will be in production, things that will themselves ensure the continued success of even seriously under-performing writers for years after their best work has been done.

Tips and Summary:

1) Good reviews have zero effect on sales.
2) Bad reviews have zero effect on sales – unless the reviews are so bad that the author brawls in public with the reviewer, in which case sales will almost certainly increase.

SECOND ONE (THE)

'For the last two weeks I have written scarcely anything. I have been idle. I have failed.'

Katherine Mansfield

People say the second book is harder than the first. The theory being that you've put tons of your energy, and probably your one big, good story into that first book, so what do you do next?

Some people, it's true, *never* get another idea, and are one-book authors. Others, (Donna Tartt: **The Secret History,** 1994; **The Little Friend,** 2002; JD Salinger: **The Catcher in the Rye,** 1951, and Joseph Heller: **Catch 22,** 1961; **Something Happened**, 1974) wait years, or even decades, for an idea for their second book.

For a lot of writers, the second book's a critical and – sometimes – commercial failure, too. Irvine Welsh could hardly fail to disappoint after the triumph of the book and film of **Trainspotting** (1993), and he didn't: **Marabou Stork Nightmares** (1996) (the title something of a clue, perhaps) was no **Trainspotting** #2.

Alex Garland's **The Beach** (1997) was followed by the disappointing (according to his fans) **The Tesseract** (1998). Again, maybe there's a clue in the title, something about very successful first book authors trying too hard?

In 2002, you'd have thought that Zadie Smith had committed some sort of imprisonable offence the way **The Autograph Man**, her second novel was received after the dazzling achievement of her first, **White Teeth** (2000).

Frank McCourt had a massive hit with his memoir **Angela's Ashes** in 1996, but failed to score in quite the same way, either critically or commercially with the follow-up, **'Tis,** in 1999. (Title clue again?)

Harper Lee quit while she was ahead and didn't try to improve upon her 1960 **To Kill a Mocking Bird**.

Another writer who sat back on her laurels – and what laurels they were – was Margaret Mitchell who wrote the fastest-selling book of all time, **Gone With The Wind,** in 1936.

Ralph Ellison, who wrote **The Invisible Man** in 1952, left his second novel, **Juneteenth,** unfinished at his death in 1994.

Whitbread winner Paul Sayer says that writing the second one's much harder than the first, and claims that in desperation, '... you'll put anything together that might fit between hard covers, that might reasonably be called a 'novel', and be ready to come out next spring.'

Michael Dobbs (**House of Cards,** 1989) agrees, 'The real test of whether you are cut out to be a writer is the second novel. The first one is written in a burst of enthusiasm, and then when you try again, you realise that writing is proper work...'

Tips and Summary:

1) Don't do it: whether it's book one or book ten, it's a miserable business, ask any writer.

SLUSH PILE

'The uncomplimentary name given to the vast quantity of unso-licited material continually delivered to publishing offices.'

Gordon Wells

This unpleasant term is one with which you are likely to become familiar. Unfortunately, with the newspapers full of ads asking readers the rhetorical question: *'Do you want to be a writer?'* and with the resounding answer to that question apparently being an almost universal, *'Yes, I most certainly do,'* until quite recently, publishers were being swamped and simply could not cope with the number of submissions.

Today, therefore, many of them have been forced to adopt a policy of not even *accepting* manuscripts for reading unless they come on very strong recommendation from an existing client or from a literary agent.

On the other hand, just about every bestselling novel of the last God knows how many years has been sent unsolicited to either a publisher or an agent (where, of course, most of them have been returned to their authors before, eventually, going on to be massive bestsellers).

But, given that of the hundred thousand plus books that were published in the UK in 2001, some seven thousand were new novels, there clearly is a problem of over-production here.

One literary agency speculated that the likelihood of finding something publishable in the slush pile was rather less than 0.001 per cent. One can only hope that they were exaggerating.

Novelist Alice Thomas Ellis (who also 'read' for her husband's company, publishers, Duckworth) wrote despairingly that she was amazed that 'people with no talent for writing at all should sit down and plong out 700 or 800 pages' simply because of their 'mad urge to be in print.'

While she took against books which contained the main character's name on the first page, 'Denis Maltravers fumbled thoughtfully with his fly buttons...', or books set in offices, her husband's methods of weeding out manuscripts that wouldn't appeal to him included rejecting anything with a covering letter that invited him to 'peruse' the enclosed.

Fact is, it's a highly subjective business, and there's no science involved at all. While the ads in the books pages might tell us that we're all writers, publishers appear more sceptical about these claims.

And there's the rub. Literary agent Juri Gabriel says that he reads as much as is necessary to make a decision, but the decision is almost always a rejection. He adds gloomily that 'those of us who sift, do so because we're temperamentally inclined to sift through piles of rubbish'.

But not everyone is so discouraging. One agent says cheerfully, 'Why should people give up? After all, so much of what is published and successful is absolute crap. Why not them?'

Surprisingly perhaps, even against these daunting odds, there are not only thousands of us toiling at the hill, moaning and groaning about conditions there, but even as we toil and groan, there are thousands more eager to join us in our quest. For, like it or not, notwithstanding the concomitant misery of our endeavours, having one's book published is still regarded in most circles with a certain amount of awe.

Do I have the answer? No, I don't. I *do* think that there are too many books in the world, just as I think that there are too many writers. I also think that the very great majority of these books do not 'need' to be written, (except, perhaps, for the purpose of exorcising some particular demons of the author, or to fulfil that writer's wish to achieve some tawdry fame or minor kudos).

Go into Borders on Oxford Street, go into a specialist bookstore such as Crime in Store in London's Bloomsbury and you, too, will be mightily depressed at the books piled and stacked and ranged before you there. Be mortified by all those titles. Be horrified at the prospect of having to read even the tiniest fraction of them, and be truly suicidal (and probably certifiably insane) if you think you want to join them.

Of course you will nurture the delusion that you will be the next John Grisham, Dave Pelzer or even Zadie Smith. But believe me, you won't. You are infinitely more likely to be the next wholly anonymous David Armstrong, a pathetic figure whose couple of titles – if you're lucky – will be hiding amongst the hundreds of thousands of jostling competitors.

Don't follow suit. Get a boat. Play golf. Improve your tennis.

If you think that this is just sour grapes from a disillusioned writer, a person whose dearest, most earnest wish was simply to be in print, this is what American novelist, Joseph Epstein, writing in the *New York Times* in September, 2002, said: 'According to a recent survey, 81% of Americans feel they have a book in them – and that they should write it. As the author of fourteen books, I'd like to do what I can to discourage them. Something of the order of 80,000 new books are published in America every year, most of them not needed, not wanted, not in any way remotely necessary... so why add to the schlock pile?'

Tips and Summary:

1) See Joseph Epstein, above. Just say No. Please, don't write that book.

TALKS

'Language most shows a man: speak, that I may see thee.'

Ben Jonson

If you want to try and sell a few of the books that you've written –
but that nobody, apparently, wants – there are a few things that
you can do. Most of them end in tears, of course. For this whole
business is the stuff of misery and humiliation.

Bookshops, even your local bookshop, can be hard to penetrate
for a midlist writer: hardbacks at nearly twenty quid a time are difficult to sell without publicity and, as a midlist novelist, it is highly unlikely that any money will have been spent on promoting
your books.

You can approach the bookshop chains (Waterstone's, Ottakar's,
Borders, Books Etc. and the like,) and ask them if they have your
book. They won't. You can ask them if they will stock your book.
They will tell you that the crime buyer is in a meeting/at lunch/in
Amsterdam for a stag weekend/at a conference.

You can leave your name and your card, but it is a cardinal rule
that neither booksellers, publishers nor agents will *ever* call you
back. Phil Redmond, creator of TV's *Brookside, Grange Hill* and
Hollyoaks, once said that the best thing about being famous is not
the Ferrari or the exotic holidays, but that people now returned his
calls. We should be so lucky.

Not surprisingly, perhaps, you feel aggrieved: how are your books
supposed to sell? Your reviews are OK, the book has a decent cover
and is nicely put together, but without some promotion and display, your novel will remain a well-kept secret. And all the time,
needless to say, the same half dozen high-profile names are promoted with full page ad's, billboards, posters and point-of-sale material.

It can seem that these blooming writers hardly need further publicity, while you are like a seed which, instead of being sown in the fecund loam of exposure, and warmed by the sunlight of a little promotion, remains sealed in the foil darkness of the packet, with no chance to grow.

Oh, well. It's a thoroughly miserable business, and I earnestly recommend you, yet again, not to do it.

But you will ignore my advice just as surely as I ignore it myself, and so, to try and up your evanescent profile, you *do* approach bookshops – with little success.

Libraries throughout the country take a few dozen copies – thank the lord for libraries – and you foist a few copies on friends. But then, to try and help your own cause, you agree to do a few 'talks'.

If a reading group or a library contacts your publisher, and they want someone from the area in which you live to give a talk or a reading, perhaps the publicity person in her London office, assuming that she even knows where you live – I'm in rural Shropshire – might give you a call.

The money's poor, of course, maybe as little as twenty or thirty pounds (if it were more, it wouldn't be *you* who was being invited) but you should always try to make yourself available for this kind of thing.

It may be the obsessive wish to be read, but my motives may be even baser than that: something about wanting to be seen, heard and liked. And whatever the reason, I tend to think that even *one* more reader is a good thing. Very sad, eh?

Prior to being a full-time writer, I was a college lecturer and so I have some experience of communicating with small groups of people. But, really, there's quite a difference between talking to your fifteen A-level students about **Sons and Lovers**, and speaking to a group whom you've never met, and who may or may not be interested in what you have to say.

On the first few occasions that I did this kind of thing – the very first one was in a tiny village library in rural Staffordshire – I stood at a table and talked for forty minutes about my work, and punctuated it with short readings.

The problem is, that you are firing off into an abyss. You have little idea whether you are actually hitting the target or not. And if there's someone at the back of the room whose eyes start to droop in the library warmth after a decent lunch, you can readily assume that everyone else is bored stiff too, and your confidence drains away.

At the end of this particular talk, far from being bored, this group of library readers asked lots of questions, applauded generously, and even bought copies of my books.

I've since done many readings and talks in bookstores, libraries and at literary get-togethers, but I now invariably opt for an interview format. It is, after all, much more natural to sit opposite someone and *discuss* matters, rather than stand up and declaim about them.

I even offer, prior to the event, to give the chairperson a list of suggested ideas for discussion. This isn't cheating. I'm perfectly happy to answer just about any question about being a writer that might come up spontaneously. But very soon, you will find that the sorts of things that most people want to know, get asked again and again: How long does it take you to write a novel? Can you live on what you make from writing? Where do you get your ideas from? Which do you concentrate on first: plot or character etc.?

These are valid and reasonable questions and they are asked repeatedly. And why not? They are exactly what *I* would want to know. Your interlocutor may have questions of his or her own. There will almost certainly be questions from the audience and, with the dozen or so that you have handed to the person sitting beside you, it should go sweetly.

Naturally, at some point, it is a good idea to give a reading from your work. I tend to keep readings very short indeed. I want to give a flavour of the work but, unless the audience has a copy of the text in front of them, people's capacity to follow what is going on in a piece of prose with little context or preparation is, I think, limited.

It is possible to distribute copies of your books to members of the audience and let them read along with you. This has risks, but I have also found that it can have real benefits. I recently did a talk for a friend who was teaching a residential course on using English for effective communication.

She had asked me to come in after dinner on the Saturday evening and give the students a bit of respite from their own writing, and an insight into the life of someone who writes fiction.

The course was in a nice, big country house in the improbably-named village of Badger, just outside Bridgnorth in Shropshire. They were a group of a dozen folk and we sat around in easy chairs in a cosy atmosphere.

I chose a self-contained passage of about two and a half pages from **Thought For The Day**.

I had just dealt with a question about where one gets ideas from, and explained that one of my sources is newspapers. I told them the story of the American banker who intended to fake his own death by driving his car into Lake Como. The plan was to have his partner collect on his (considerable) life insurance.

In fact, due to a problem with the central locking, the man failed to escape from the car, and was eventually found (dead) half out of the rear window at the bottom of the lake. His 'escape kit' of a motorcycle and rucksack full of dry clothes was subsequently found on a nearby wooded hillside.

The story was macabre, ironic and tragic. The Italian police solved the intended crime in about fifteen seconds: the car had left the road on a straight piece of tarmac; there were no signs of braking and, because this was one of the very few places where the lakeside road was straight, there were no barriers to impede the car's plunge. Also, the car was a Mercedes. I had kept the story filed for some ten years.

When I began **Thought For The Day**, I intended to use a version of the story of the American banker's tragic death as the ending of the book, even though, at that time, I had little idea of exactly how I was going to get there.

I showed the group the newspaper story and then handed out paperback copies of my book and read with them my fictionalised account of it. They were very complimentary about the way I had adapted and informed the newspaper story with my own speculation about what those terrible minutes might have been like for the drowning man.

Having the book in their hands as I read to them, they had a direct, tactile connection with it and were then loath, I suspect, to part with it. It wasn't a calculatedly mercenary plan, but it's a fact that nearly everyone in the room then bought a copy of the book that they were holding.

More recently I did a talk for an organisation called U3A. I'd never heard of them before, but it stands for University of the Third Age, (the 'third age' being that of senior citizens).

It was held one Thursday morning at the Memorial Hall in the market town where I live.

My next door neighbour, who is a member, had put my name forward as a speaker, and they had booked me for a small fee. The money's neither here nor there. Writing's a solitary pursuit – which is one of the reasons I like it – but it *is* nice to get out of the house now and again, and to have the experience of meeting people who are interested in what it is you do. It never fails to give me a warm glow.

When I got to the Memorial Hall, rather than the dozen people I had expected, there were about a *hundred*. I arranged my books

211

on the table and the chairperson proceeded to deal with the notices for the next couple of weeks.

The art appreciation group would be visiting the Lowry in Manchester; places were still available for the art trip to Bruges in July.

Next month the literature group would be meeting in Mr Jones's house when the topic for discussion would be Strindberg's influence on European drama in the early part of the 20th century.

I looked around for a hidden camera. Was this some sort of elaborate joke? I thought I was here to coast through half an hour of chatting to a few OAPs about being a crime writer, and maybe sell half a dozen paperbacks, not speak in front of an erudite, large audience of well-read people who appeared to be in their fifties.

I did my stuff: gave my 'interview', and a couple of short readings. The question and answer session that followed was buoyant, the audience alert and interested.

At the end, the applause was warm and I actually had to try and maintain some sort of order as I was besieged by members of the audience. I sold all the books that I had brought with me, and took orders for several more.

I felt like Eric Clapton when he's just played solo at the Royal Albert Hall!

This summer, I've taken part in half a dozen talks in the *Read Routes* programme, a London-wide series of crime panels organised by London Libraries.

I've played Hammersmith (the library, not the Odeon), and Upminster. Upminster is at the end of the District Line, and the end of the District Line is just about the end of the world as we know it. It's not even *in* London, it's in Essex…

But no matter, the audience seemed pleased that intrepid crime writers had journeyed through Plaistow and Dagenham and all points east to share with them our thoughts on topics such as: 'Do women or men make the best fictional detectives?'

I also went to Hounslow. If you ever get to Hounslow, it's so far west, you might as well visit friends in America as come back to Primrose Hill.

The last panel I did, in the middle of September, was with stand-up comedian turned crime writer and TV dramatist, Marc Blake, and music agent and Camden-based crime novelist, Paul Charles. The moderator was the *Observer's* crime fiction critic, Peter Guttridge.

This last gig was in Bow. (I'd never been there before, either.)

When I got off the tube at Mile End, there was one of those big yellow police boards that are such a depressingly familiar sight in London these days. This one was asking for witnesses to a murder that had happened the previous week. On the platform of Mile End tube. At *five* o'clock. In the evening.

Immediately outside the station, there were several, 'Be warned, you are now in a mugging area,' boards. I walked briskly through the streets of (pleasant) villas, and arrived at the library with five minutes to spare.

The library was situated in a shopping centre. But unlike my local supermarket, at the door of this one were two hefty guys in security garb.

We three invited writers did the talk. The subject was: 'Crime fiction: safety valve or incitement?' The audience numbered five more than were on the panel, and that included the reliably-supportive organiser from London libraries, Natasha Innocent.

(Should you be wishing that you had been there, I can report that the consensus was that very few criminals decide to kill someone simply because they have read a novel about murder – malice generally having been hatched with a deal of aforethought.

We did, though, think that some criminals might pick up the odd tip on trying to fox the police – they certainly need all the help they can get these days in the unequal struggle to get away with murder, given the sophistication of forensic science.

People pick up from crime novels all sorts of information, and I dare say that the average reader of Patricia Cornwell can, if they've been paying attention, perform at least a routine autopsy.

It was also suggested that while *reading* crime fiction might not provide a safety valve, *writing* it sometimes does. Writing **Until Dawn Tomorrow** certainly helped me cope with the trauma of a separation and divorce. I doubt that I would have *murdered* my ex-wife's lover, but to channel some of the angst of that period into a novel was, I think, pretty cathartic.)

We chatted about this and that, took questions, had a glass of wine, and were escorted out of the building by the security guards.

Writers talk big about crime and criminals, but this writer's liver is distinctly lily. It's now ten o'clock, the streets are dark and, if the big yellow boards are to be believed, in these parts people get murdered as early as five in the evening.

Peter Guttridge is a good six-foot-three, and he led, Natasha by his side. I stuck with Marc Blake and the girl he claimed was his stalker; Paul and a chum brought up the rear. In this defensive column we marched resolutely back to the tube station.

Read Routes was a fantastic success. We went to unusual places and met enthusiastic audiences who don't often get to hear writers. Of course, there were some well-established authors, Natasha Cooper, Simon Brett, Stella Duffy and Nicolas Blincoe, as well as rising stars, Elizabeth Woodcraft, Marc Blake and Mark Billingham, but many of the high-profile names were either on book tours or not tempted by the thirty quid a time appearance money, so we midlist writers got a look in.

A couple of years ago, midlist writer Margaret Murphy, despairing of her publisher funding any kind of publicity for her books, had the bright idea of putting together a few writers and doing talks and appearances as a group.

The benefits were obvious. Not only is there a camaraderie in numbers (there's nothing worse than appearing at the library or wherever and finding just yourself and the caretaker) but with four or five of you in the group, you can advertise your wares more brazenly (after all, it's easier to shamefacedly promote a group of which you are a part, rather than simply selling yourself).

Also, the group will have different strengths, both in terms of what they are writing and how they interact with audiences. And of course, an audience coming to see one writer might well then develop an interest in reading another member's work.

All in all, a thoroughly good idea.

It's been a huge success, and groups of writers like One Over the Eight, Rogues and Vagabonds, Ox-blood, LadyKillers and the original group, Murder Squad are now a regular feature of festivals and literary hoedowns. If you're a big name and can draw a crowd, by all means, go solo, but for midlist writers, this is an excellent way of getting out, meeting other writers, and probably lots more readers, too.

Tips and summary:

1) Say yes to doing talks.
2) Photocopy what you're going to read for members of the audience or, even better, distribute copies of the paperback you're reading from.
3) Keep readings short.
4) Consider forming a group of writers to take your work out.

TV ... AND BOOKS

'No one is going to sit down and read **Bleak House** *to the family any more, but they can all huddle up happily in front of Charles Bronson.'*

Martin Amis

A midlist writer might sell a few thousand copies of his or her book. I have several friends who write for TV. A mainstream TV drama series might be seen by anything up to fifteen or sixteen million viewers. They naturally get very well paid for their work. The writer's fee is, after all, only a tiny part of the budget when making an hour's TV.

But, in spite of the big cheques and the huge viewing figures for TV, there is still something wonderful and unique about producing a book. It's durable; it's all your own work; it's there on the shelf, and you can get it down, handle it and, heaven forbid, even re-read it. (Personally, I rarely do, apart from that stomach-churning moment when you read the first printed copy, knowing that it's now too late to fix that clunky sentence in chapter three, or change the colour of the car that's green in chapter nine and has somehow become blue in chapter thirty.)

In a dozen years, the book will still be there. On readers' shelves; in the Oxfam shop, maybe; in the local library (if the maniac with the blue biro hasn't rendered it unreadable by deleting every single profanity).

And so, yes, although there's simply no comparison to be made between numbers of readers and numbers of viewers – and I wish *I* was earning TV-writing dosh instead of tiny advances – there *is* something special about a book. That fanning through of new paper, the slip of the cover, the weight of the thing, the very text on the page.

217

And of course, you wrote all those words yourself – they're not for someone else to deliver on film and swap and change. It's your name on the spine; your name on the cover. And it'll stay there, it doesn't roll off the screen with the name of the best boy, the gaffer and the second unit director. These are very small things, I hear you say. And yes, they are. But they're kind of nice, too.

God knows, there must be *some* reason why we do it!

Tips and Summary:

1) If you want the money, write for TV.
2) If you want to be miserable, but to own something you can cradle in your lap, or (heaven forbid) get down from the shelf and show your children, write a book.

UNPLEASANTNESS

'Even if my marriage is falling apart and my children are unhappy, there is still a part of me that says, 'God, this is fascinating!'
Jane Smiley

It's been said that 90 per cent of fiction is autobiography. It's hardly surprising, then, that writers often use their books to pay off scores and dish the dirt. I know I do. It's a perfect opportunity: all the arguments, all the affronts done to you, outlined and articulated, and not a dissenting voice allowed. The other person/people traduced for their short-sightedness, their stupidity, their bad breath and inadequate sexuality. It almost makes the whole miserable exercise worthwhile. Almost.

Of course, there's a price to be paid: you will lose friends, family, lovers, partners and colleagues. DH Lawrence and Jessie Chambers; Margaret Drabble and AS Byatt; Hanif Kureishi and the mother of his children; Charles Dickens and Leigh Hunt; Rebecca West and HG Wells, the list is endless.

People will invariably be hurt to see themselves described in (frequently unflattering) ways in the pages of your novel. Your book's integrity may mean everything to *you*, but don't expect *them* to be quite so forgiving merely for *your* art's sake. They won't be.

I've frequently deluded myself in this regard, thinking that my own enthusiasm for my work would naturally be shared by the very people whom I have offended there.

In fact, even more tragically, having been a total social and academic misfit at school and throughout my teenage years, I actually thought, when I found, in my twenties, that I could write, that this would somehow be my redemption. That because I had discovered some facility in this area, I would now be, if not admired, then at least liked and respected.

Of course, nothing could have been further from the truth. The few people who had liked and respected me continued to do so, and the rest of the world maintained its indifference or, worse, resented what little success I had, and dismissed it as a fluke.

More pointedly, as one ex-friend remarked to me, summing up what I thought of as a reasonable achievement – five novels in eight years – 'No one likes a smart-arse.'

I once wrote a short piece about a cycling holiday that I took with a colleague and his teenage son. The boy moaned and whined the whole time, and when the *Sunday Times Travel Book* published the account a few months later, I showed it to my friend, hoping (anticipating, even) that he would equally enjoy my witty observations about we three ill-sorted folk pedalling through Brittany.

Now, Daniel may not have been the most attentive of fathers, and he was a serial philanderer to boot, but how could I possibly expect any father to applaud such a barbed depiction of his son?

But I did. Surprisingly, amazingly, he didn't hit me. In fact, we remained (sort of) friends until he finally left the marital home a few years later and started a new life with a recently-widowed childhood sweetheart.

In another remarkably inept piece of self-delusion, I once wrote a story about some dodgy operators who ran a second-hand car lot on the corner of the street where I used to live.

All *I* could see in my couple of thousand words (possibly to be used as half a chapter in some future, yet-to-be-written book) were my insightful, funny observations about these minor criminals and the way they conducted their business.

But surely only an extraordinarily deluded individual would present these wily (and slightly dangerous) car dealers with the piece for their diversion. Which is exactly what I did.

Again, they didn't hit me, but they did look at me askance as they exchanged baffled glances between themselves.

It wasn't long after this that I had my nervous breakdown.

My worst offence of this sort, though, concerns my own father. Mum was always encouraging Dad to make visits to his grown-up children. Dad reluctantly obliged, spending days of his holidays on National Express buses, even though he would much rather have been sat in his own front room watching the Channel Four racing or having a game of snooker with his mates.

Twenty years ago, Dad came on a visit when we lived in the Shropshire countryside. Glowing about the perspicacity of my observations about my own childhood and family in a recently written piece, I offered Dad a chunk of it. He took the manuscript up to bed with him.

When I came down the next morning, he was gone. Dad was an easy-going man, and not really demonstrative at all. He'd torn a strip off the top of the Cornflakes box and written a terse, hurt farewell. We lived up a long dirt track at the end of a meandering lane three miles from the town. Dad didn't drive a car. He had really wanted to go.

I didn't see him again for six months; he refused to speak to me on the phone. I think it brought him and Mum closer together, but that was little comfort to me for the hurt I had foolishly done to him.

A lot of writers feel a need to pay off old scores, and much of the vitriol and spite of these feelings finds its way into your first book. This book is not your first *published* book, but your first *written* book. It's often known as the 'bottom-drawer' book. And that's exactly where it should be. Although there are exceptions to this rule, most of us simply pour our undiluted bile and vanity into that first work.

The hero is invariably a sensitive and perceptive soul, a person blessed with insight and good looks, who is a caring and successful lover, an attentive companion, and wiser than all of the people with whom he works, plays football or socialises.

While *they* are robust, conniving and shallow, he is vulnerable, innocent and misunderstood by an ungrateful and uncaring world.

This book should be consigned to the bottom drawer of the filing cabinet and only looked at again for the purposes of self-flagellation.

It is in subsequent books that glancing blows, poking jabs and wounding upper cuts can be delivered, but they should be more measured, less overt, and more subtle.

In Hanif Kureishi's short novel, **Intimacy** (1998) the writer describes leaving the mother of his two boys for another woman. Kureishi writes of drinking champagne and having sex and strawberries with his lover while his wife sorts out appointments with a therapist to try and refloat their beached marriage.

Now, I think I've a pretty fair understanding of the sliver of ice that Graham Greene claimed resides in the heart of every writer, but did Kureishi *really* need to crucify her like this? Why? What was the imperative? His wife had done him no harm, he says. He had simply tired of her and their relationship.

She must have been tortured by these revelations. What was his rationale? It's the old **Sons and Lovers** debate: Lawrence tells his tale; his devoted friend, Jessie Chambers, is left to pick up the pieces and rue the betrayal of herself and her family by the man she has loved, and whose work and being she has nurtured.

Jessie Chambers wrote her own account of the events described in **Sons and Lovers**, but few people, of course, were interested. 'Never trust the artist, trust the tale,' said Lawrence, and it is *his* **Sons and Lovers** that remains, no matter how unfair and brutal it must have been for the people who felt betrayed by the story on its pages.

Tips and Summary:

1) Writers should come with a health warning: approach with extreme caution.

VANITY (AND SELF-) PUBLISHING

'From the moment I picked it up, until the moment I laid it down, I was convulsed with laughter. Some day I intend reading it.'

Groucho Marx

A lot of people feel that they have a story to tell. Often, it's the case that, at a certain time of life, they feel a wish to leave a record of the things that they've done and seen. A lot of successful books, of course, spring from exactly this sort of impetus. The question is, does what you have to say, what you have seen and thought and felt, have wider application? Will it be of interest to readers beyond your immediate circle of friends, acquaintances and family?

If you're going to write a book that's going to tap into experience that can in some sense be described as universal, you are going to have readers. Or perhaps you have something unique to impart. If you are one of the few people to have travelled to the moon or spent years in a foreign prison or survived a plane crash, you will have something to say that's unique, exciting and engaging.

Of course, the internal journey, though, is the one that most people travel: it's their *thoughts* and *feelings,* the unique way in which they perceive the commonplace that makes their tale universal. After all, James Joyce's Leopold Bloom is simply a Dublin advertisement canvasser who relates the events of a June day in 1904.

Most people's experience of love, work and family is probably no more dramatic and exciting than Leopold Bloom's in **Ulysses** or Paul Morel's in Lawrence's **Sons and Lovers**. These characters don't travel to exotic places, do little more than fight, struggle with their art, make love, mourn their loved ones. So, it is not the facts of the story that are significant, it's simply the ability of these writers to imbue their stories with the imaginative richness that makes us chime with our own (possibly similar) notions of the things described.

No wonder then, at a certain time of life, people who have worked down a mine, run a big company or a corner shop, travelled to the east, taken drugs, had love affairs, lost loved ones, or faced illness and grief themselves, feel that they, too, want to tell their story.

Often, though, unlike Joyce and Lawrence, these people are not writers. Sometimes, it's clear that they are not readers either.

The fact is, if you want to publish your life story – or, indeed, some other story that you think is viable – go ahead and try. But if you find difficulty in interesting a mainstream publisher you might be encouraged to respond to one of the ads that appear in little boxes in the Sunday papers, saying that here is a company who actually *wants* to publish your work.

You can be forgiven for contacting them.

They are, invariably, vanity publishers. They don't, of course, give themselves such a pejorative title. But this is what they are. Appealing to the vanity of the writer, they will offer to publish your book, and they will do it. It'll cost you, of course. Many thousands of pounds. Book publishing is an expensive business, and all publishers, both bona fide ones and the so-called vanity publishers, are in business to make money. You send your manuscript to Minerva or The Book Guild and, in only a week or two's time, you will receive a letter telling you that the editor has enjoyed your manuscript (there will probably be specific reference to your book, its subject matter, even the characters and plot – which are beautiful things to read after the months and, possibly, years of neglect and indifference – and that they are prepared to publish it).

You then have the sobering experience of reading the terms and conditions of its publication. It will cost, depending upon how many words there are in your manuscript, and how many copies you would like to be printed, between four and eight thousand pounds.

They will try and distribute it for you (there are no guarantees about this, of course) and you will be consulted about the artwork, typeface, cover etc.

At least the companies mentioned above, whilst never actually calling themselves 'vanity' publishers, make no pretence of the fact that they are only prepared to publish your book if you are willing to pay. But beware, there are less upfront operators in the market, too.

An acquaintance of mine who has published many short stories and some magazine fiction has been trying to get his novel read by a bona fide publisher for nearly a year now.

This is not a deluded youngster, with no idea of how the market works or which sort of publishing house might be interested in the kind of 'commercial' novel which (he believes) he has written. But the fact is, whether he's the next Nick Hornby or not, he just cannot get the book read.

He has recently been approaching smaller publishers with his book.

One publisher in particular has been in correspondence with him for a couple of months now.

It's a masterclass in the art of drawing in the 'mark'. The early letters were quite equivocal in their response to his pitch, but gave just enough encouragement (and no mention of a reading fee or contribution to publishing costs) to elicit from him further enquiries.

They apparently read the manuscript and claimed to have discussed it at editorial meetings and were now considering publishing it. Nothing too rushed or fulsome here.

They then bemoaned the state of the market, the great costs involved in publishing first novels, and suggested that it 'may be necessary to ask for a small contribution from you,' were they to go ahead.

Even at this point, they are asking for a financial commitment 'in principle' with no mention of the amount, and a caveat that even if he were to agree to put up money, they 'cannot promise... to proceed.'

This is clever. They're not (apparently) falling over themselves for his money, nor are they claiming he's Proust. It's also true that the costs and returns on first novels are prohibitive. It's almost too much for a desperate author to resist.

But my friend is resisting: the most recent letter that he has received has asked him for a 'contribution' of £3,675. A contract is enclosed with the letter. It makes no mention of the number of copies that would be printed, or how they would be distributed. There is a reference to 'promotion', but my friend suspects that this might be no more than a mention of his putative novel on the company's internet site.

So, if you have a spare few thousand pounds, if you are desperate to see your book in print, and want to give copies to friends and family and try to sell a few to your mates at the pub or squash club, then go ahead. Just do be fully aware, though, of what it is that you are signing up for.

You may believe that you have written a book that deserves to be seen by a wider public, and you might be right. But the fact that a bona fide publisher is not prepared to pay even a miserly advance of a thousand or two, should be seen as not only publishers' ignorance, short-sightedness and ill-breeding, but that they may just be right.

Not necessarily, of course. We know only too well how many mistakes are made. But it *is* a possibility, and after all, they are still in business, and against all the odds in this multi-media, short attention-span world, they are still making a profit by selling books. It is, therefore, just worth considering that they, not you, might be right. I know how hard this is to accept.

My advice would be to think about what it is that you have written and, if you don't read much yourself, do you think that you have the requisite skills to have written a novel?

After all, would you offer to build a house, having once put up three wonky courses of a garden wall? Or play for England having had a kick-around in the park?

If, after all this consideration, you still want to see yourself in print, then sure, go ahead. Get your dosh out of the Halifax and sign up. You might well be pleased and proud of your book when it emerges from the presses.

But unless you can persuade a few local outlets to stock a couple on sale or return, it won't be appearing in bona fide bookshops no matter how hard you try and sell it. Forget it appearing in Waterstone's or Smith's, because it won't; forget libraries buying it, because they won't, and save your postage on sending it to the literary editors of anything but the most provincial of newspapers, because they definitely won't review it.

But at the very least, they'll make nice Christmas and birthday presents for the family, and you'll be able to read yourself, 'in print'.

Self-publishing, as opposed to vanity publishing, has a more noble, not to say eccentric tradition. Any number of writers, from William Blake, Lawrence Sterne to Walt Whitman, Virginia Woolf and DH Lawrence have published themselves.

In 1988 Jill Paton Walsh could not find a publisher to take on her **Knowledge of Angels** and, believing in her book, she decided to publish it at her own expense. She was vindicated when the novel was selected for the Booker Prize shortlist of that year.

In 1996, prize-winning author Timothy Mo, dissatisfied with his publisher's offer for his new novel, published **Brownout on Breadfruit** himself.

JL Carr (**A Month in the Country,** 1980), was twice shortlisted for the Booker Prize. Carr had seven novels published in the conventional way, but as well as writing fiction, the ex-headmaster self-published a series of handy 16-page booklets featuring the work of poets and miscellaneous figures from sport and history.

The success of this little series, (which anticipated the **Penguin 60's** booklets by several years) was crucial when it came to self-publishing his last novel, **What Hetty Did,** in 1988. Carr already had contact with a network of some two hundred bookshops and was therefore able, with the help of an enthusiastic sales rep., to distribute his novel with relative ease. Apparently, he even made a profit on it.

Tips and Summary:

1) As a last resort, if you can't get anyone to buy (or even read) your book, consider self- or vanity-publishing it.
2) Either way, you'll only sell three copies, and it'll cost you a fortune.
3) Better still, don't do it

WAITING

'Life is a horizontal fall.'

Jean Cocteau

Time is the thing. In publishing – and even more so, in *non*-publishing – time is elastic. They reckon it can take easily five years to get a movie off the ground. Richard Attenbrough took *twenty* years to raise the cash and get *Gandhi* made, and Martin Scorsese nearly as long to make *Gangs of New York*.

Books aren't usually this bad, but even for people like me, people writing modest books with modest aims, it's nothing for a book to take two or three years to get published, even after it's been written. If you're lucky.

When my first book was published, in November 1993, my wife gave me at Christmas a copy of the **Writers' and Artists' Yearbook**. After the years of submitting manuscripts, my previous copies of the guide were dog-eared and heavily annotated.

Julia wrote in the flyleaf: 'Congratulations! You won't be needing this again.' (Sadly, it didn't turn out to be true, but it was a typically sweet and thoughtful message.)

The thing about trying to get published is that it really is – for most of us – a very time-consuming business. You write the book (which is often pretty hard, of course) and then you have to embark on the truly terrible time of writing letters, sending emails and making telephone calls trying to persuade supposedly interested people to even look at it.

Simon Gray, a man who has written over twenty stage plays, lots of TV films, a couple of movies and five novels, is still painfully familiar with this syndrome. He writes in **Enter a Fox**, his 2001 account of the particular miseries associated with being a playwright, that he sat at his desk, 'not so much worn out by the task

231

completed as drained in advance by the task ahead ... sending it (the play) out, waiting for responses ... this, for me, is the truly ghastly part of playwriting, and the prospect of it somehow taints the work itself.'

As a little-known novelist, if someone eventually deigns to agree to look at your book, you send it off, and then wait two, three or four months.

Eventually, you call.

The last thing you want to do is provoke an intemperate reaction. The editor of your dreams will have slipped off his barbour jacket one Sunday afternoon, might have had a glass of wine after a good lunch and a walk with his red-setter, and to have read in a leisurely but deeply interested manner a few chapters of your fascinating novel.

In reality, after the months of waiting, you gird your loins and make the most cowering telephone enquiry of some Aussie temp on the end of the line in a central London office.

Nudged into a response, your would-be publisher/editor might, at this point, between faxes, meetings and calls from equally hungry and desperate authors, finally skim a few pages of your book.

And then, almost certainly, she will troll off a note telling her secretary to draft a letter to Ms Rowling to the effect that, whilst the author's manuscript is not without a certain something, regrettably, in these commercially-driven times, there is no market for tales of orphaned schoolboys attending wizard schools.

To a Mr Rankin of Edinburgh, she writes that, in a competitive crime market that is positively awash with misanthropic, jazz-loving, heavy-drinking, maverick detectives, she sees no place for his creation, the dour 'John Rebus'.

By the same post – what a good feeling it is to make some small impression on the ever-growing pile of manuscripts that threatens to overwhelm her office – she fires off a missive to a young man called Oliver, explaining to the poor, garrulous mutt, that the cookery-book market has been sewn up by Delia Smith, Rick Stein and, in any event, has been basted to death.

Your own novel comes back four days later, the solitary hair that you placed between pages twenty-three and-four is, just as you knew it would be, still there.

You want to phone. You want to tell them you have caught them out in their shoddy, dastardly non-reading trick. Instead, you turn up the **Writers' and Artists' Yearbook**, call the next publisher on the list and begin the whole miserable, dispiriting process over again.

All this takes tons of time, is absolutely debilitating and wrecks any shred of confidence in your work that you might still have.

Tips and Summary:

1) Believe me, hard though it often is, writing's actually the easy bit.
2) Don't do it.

XYLOPHONE

'A percussion instrument consisting of a set of wooden bars of graduated length. It is played with hard-headed hammers.'
Collins Concise Dictionary

Even time spent playing one of these will seem like time well spent compared with writing a book and trying to get it published.

Tips and Summary:

1) Join a band
2) Play the xylophone
30) Just don't write a book

YOUTH … AND AGE

'The long day wanes: the slow moon climbs:'

Alfred Tennyson: Ulysses

In July 2002, eighteen-year-old New Yorker, Nick McDonell published his first book, **Twelve**. (Well, let's hope it was his *first* book. Or does he have a bottom drawer novel, too? Something he knocked off at kindergarten while the other kids were having their milk and rusks.)

McDonell wrote the book when he was seventeen. It's a New York-based tale of rich kids and their doings. And their doings are pretty familiar: drugs, girls, rich parents, and wanting to be black. The usual.

Two years earlier, after fourteen manuscripts and fifty *years* of rejection slips, seventy-three-year-old Daphne Anson's **Family Portraits** was published by Hamilton.

It may well be that Daphne Anson is not the writer that young McDonell is, but the septuagenarian's book was reviewed little (I could find only two entries on the internet today) and the features that I read about her at the time of publication concentrated on her age and her perseverance; novelty items, really.

McDonell's age was also mentioned, of course, but he and his novel featured widely in the media (and there are over eight *hundred* entries on him on the web today).

The consensus was that the young man had written a pretty decent book, no matter what his age, but also that youth is sexy, and sex sells.

Age is not sexy. No one's to blame, it's just a fact.

The precocious talent of McDonell was always going to stand him in good stead, of course, but so is the fact that his mother is a novelist, his father an editor with *Rolling Stone* magazine, and his godfather also happens to be his publisher.

But the book is good, and when I heard him interviewed on Radio Four's *Front Row*, he sounded like a New Yorker par-excellence: funny, bright, self-assured and totally unfazed. There was even an acknowledgement of his parents' contribution to his success, and a deal of modesty about his precocious achievement.

The publication of **Twelve** happened shortly after I had struggled to find a publisher for my new book, having been dropped by HarperCollins.

No one said it to me, but there *were* a couple of occasions when I was trying to place the book when I did feel that my age (mid-fifties), was not entirely out of the decision-making equation.

The thinking appears to be: how old is this writer, and how many books has he got left in him/her?

Equally important, I suppose, is the question of just how 'hungry' you are perceived to be. When my first book was published, I was in my mid-forties, and I was very hungry indeed. I was *ravenous*. I'm still keen, and I still want to be out there but, truth to tell, I don't have the same hunger. I know I don't.

Is this because, (on a very modest level) I've done it, with five books of fiction published and a non-fiction book written? Or is it that now I'm a little older, the whole business looks a bit vainglorious, and aspiring to success in it can look rather foolish?

So, perhaps it's fair that publishers should look on authors like myself a little askance, as they wonder just whether we will be knocked into shape, come up with the next book on time, or exhibit a bit of argy bargy if things don't go our way. After all, sad to say, we're closer to checking out than checking in, and pushed too hard just might say if things get tough: I can't really be *bothered*.

And then, of course, there's the question of justice. As ever, dross sells, and good work is frequently overlooked. Give or take half a dozen extraordinary titles, who cares about the other five or six thousand new novels that are published each year? Unless you're looking for a holiday read or a bit of beachside diversion, really, who cares about the next Ben Elton, Tony Parsons or Jeffrey Archer?

Putting together a newspaper article on a local writer friend a year or two ago, I interviewed a chum who writes for TV. We know each other well, and I just had to put on a slightly different hat to ask her a few things that, as friends, I'd never asked her before.

I got her CV and her educational background etc. and we wrapped it up over a couple of drinks. When I asked her how old she was, she said, 'Look, do you mind. I'm fifty, but would you mind not mentioning it in the piece. People working in TV are very age-sensitive. They like to work with young people, people with young outlooks, and everyone's scared of seeming too old. Do you mind?'

In 1983, the literary magazine **Granta** published a list of the hot young (under 40) writers of the day, the coming folk. It was a prescient list with Barnes and Amis, Rushdie and McEwan just some of the luminaries there.

The magazine did the same thing in 1993, (Jeanette Winterson, Will Self and Hanif Kureishi, amongst others) and this year's is just out. We'll have to wait and see just who fulfils their promise.

Radio Four's *Front Row*, looking for an amusing angle inspired by the forthcoming **Granta** list, did a piece about older (over 70) writers who tend to get overlooked in this apparent homage to youth.

Doris Lessing is 84; William Trevor 75; John Mortimer 80; PD James 83; VS Naipaul 71; Brian Aldiss 78; JG Ballard 73; Philip Callow 78; Francis King 79, and Sybille Bedford is 92.

Annie Proulx (**That Old Ace in the Hole**, 2003) had her first novel, **Postcards** (1992) published at the age of fifty-six.

239

Claire Tomalin, who didn't write her first book until she was forty, won the Whitbread non-fiction prize for **Samuel Pepys: The Unequalled Self,** in 2003 at the age of sixty-nine.

Tomalin's husband, Michael Frayn, seventy, won the Whitbread fiction prize the same year with his novel, **Spies.**

Only a month after Daphne Anson's breakthrough into print with her **Family Portraits** (2000), writer Nicholas Wollaston wrote in the *Observer* that his new novel had just been declined by his publisher, a part of the Random House group.

Unlike Anson, Wollaston had published seven novels and half a dozen non-fiction titles stretching back forty years. His publishers include Hodder, Cape, Hamish Hamilton, Constable and Deutsch.

His editor at Random House wrote to his agent saying that she liked his book, **Man in the Net** 'enormously'. She went on to say, though, that she could not publish, 'given all the standard arguments about it being late in the author's career etc.'

Wollaston, not surprisingly, felt a little miffed and had some salty things to say about young (women, mostly) who are offered big advances even though they have no track record in writing fiction, just so long as they have a pretty face for the book's cover.

And, as he rightly claims, no publisher would *dare* to turn a book down claiming race or gender, so why age?

Wollaston may be 74, but his heartfelt complaint that, 'I'm only half alive, a sort of zombie, if I'm not working on a book,' will be painfully familiar to many writers.

Tips and Summary:

1) Youth: Good.
2) Age: bad.
3) Don't do it…at any age.

ZEN ... AND THE ART OF WRITING

Try to remain calm whilst writing and – usually rather worse – trying to sell your book to a publisher/agent.

One of the best ways to achieve this is to practise Zen Buddhism.

However, if practised properly, you should soon recognise your undertaking for what it is: a shallow, obsessive, ego-fuelled wish to impress your peers, friends and colleagues with your achievement. Accepting this, you can then abandon the venture, and devote yourself to the Eight Noble Truths and following the true path to enlightenment.

If you are merely *faking* your study and meditation, though, sitting cross-legged and chanting a couple of times a day might help you to remain partially sane while writing, and then sending out your manuscript.

Then, when (if) you get the call that you have been secretly praying for, you can abandon your sitting position, rush out of the room shouting with joy and get very drunk.

Tips and Summary:

1) Be a monk.
2) Be anything.
3) *Don't* be a writer.

INDEX

245

250

254